Tickle Your Soul

Live Well,
Love Much,
Laugh Often

Anne Bryan Smollin

SORIN BOOKS   Notre Dame, IN

First printing, May 1999
Fifth printing, July 2006
26,500 copies in print

© 1999 by Sorin Books

All rights reserved. No part of this book may be used or reproduced in
any manner whatsoever, except in the case of reprints in the context of
reviews, without written permission from Sorin Books, P.O. Box 1006,
Notre Dame, IN 46556-1006.

www.sorinbooks.com

ISBN-10 1-893732-00-2 ISBN-13 978-1-893732-00-1

Library of Congress Catalog Card Number: 99-62068
Cover and text design by Maurine R. Twait
Printed and bound in the United States of America.

Contents

Introduction

There is a modern story told of the Sufi teacher and holy fool Mullah Nasrudin. He goes into a bank and tries to cash a check. The teller asks him please to identify himself. Nasrudin reaches into his pocket and pulls out a small mirror. Looking into it, he says, "Yep, that's me all right."

We all need to grow into the kind of awareness and confidence where we know—and are comfortable with—who we are. Sometimes, that is not an easy journey. Sometimes, it takes years. What matters is that we begin that journey and take small steps each day toward our goal.

Life has taught us, wrongly, that everything is easy. If we have a pain, we take a pill. If we need cash, we use our credit cards or an ATM. If we have only a few minutes to cook dinner, we use our microwaves. Cellular phones, E-mail, and personal beepers allow us instant contact with other people. As a result, when it takes work, thought, or investment of self to get something accomplished, we find ourselves looking at a concrete wall (rather than in a mirror) and thinking that the task is too difficult or even impossible.

But happiness and joy are within our reach. They are gifts and blessings and words spoken—and, yes, even unspoken. The problem is not that this state of happiness is unreachable or beyond us. The problem is that we wait for someone else to give it to us, to create our happiness and pleasure.

A Chinese proverb says: "A person without a smiling face must not open a shop." That makes sense—a smile creates warmth, hospitality, and openness. Hence, a shop owner with a smile is more successful than a glum shop owner. Who wants to be waited on by a grumpy salesperson? Who wants to live with a person who is not happy? Who wants to work with someone who is negative?

Research tells us if we smile long enough, the smile turns to laughter. We know if we tell ourselves something often enough, we begin to believe it. The same is true for smiles.

In the Koran, it is written: "They deserve paradise who make their companions laugh." What life and energy we give to others, and what energy and life others can give to us! We ease one another's burdens and carry one another's sorrows. We share one another's loads.

There is a wonderful old Russian tale about the inhabitants of heaven and hell. They both sit at tables loaded with delicious food. The ground rules for the feast are simple: the diners must eat with extremely long-handled forks, and they must grasp the forks at the end of the handle. The people in hell starve because they cannot figure out how to feed themselves that way. But for the people in heaven, this is not a problem. They simply reach across the table and feed each other.

When we realize that we were created to be social beings, that we need others and others need us, then we find fullness in life. We become aware of the connectedness of all things: the earth, the sun, the moon, the stars, the grass, the water, the dirt, the animals, the people we know and those we have not yet had the opportunity to meet. Nothing is separate. When we experience that awareness, we find ourselves praising all living and non-living things. Then we are not just experiencing joy but extending that joy to others. The connectedness of life goes on.

How true it is that we get ourselves so busy and into so many "things" and activities that we do not take the time to see the presence of joy right in front of us. Alice Walker paints with her words that reminder in her novel *The Color Purple*.

At one point, Celie and Shug are in earnest conversation about God when Shug corrects Celie's vision of how God manages the universe. Life is not, as Celie thinks, a matter of scurrying about doing good deeds to earn God's approval. It is, rather, taking time to notice, appreciate, and praise what God has provided for our pleasure and enjoyment. "I think it pisses God off if you walk by the color purple in a field somewhere and don't notice it," Shug counsels.

This book is a result of a lot of things: some people encouraging me to write it, other people challenging me to finish it, workshops and lectures I've given on this topic, and even messages that have hit me along the way. All of these things have been like signposts on the paths we walk, and not to acknowledge them or hear them would be like walking by the color purple in a field somewhere and not noticing it.

One day that was more hectic than most provided the final shove that made me take the time to complete this volume. I had several client appointments, and sand-wiched in between them were two workshops and a din-ner keynote address. The day before had been even more pressured. So when I jumped in my car after having seen five clients and given the first workshop to a hospice group on "Wellness and Humor," I began feeling very tired.

Trying to ignore this feeling because I still had to see one more client and then give the dinner address, I steered my car onto the New York State Thruway and began talking out loud to myself. I asked myself why I was working so hard and why I was accepting more speaking commitments. I began to talk about the unfinished projects I had not gotten to. Then I engaged God in my conversation: "God, why am I doing all of this? What should I do and what should I let go of? You know, God, I do enjoy working, and I love all the lectures I give. But I can't keep up this pace much longer. And what about that book? Should I finish it or should I just forget the whole thing? God, if only you would help. If only you could send me a sign, then I would know what I really should be doing."

As I said those words, I looked at the truck in front of me. The back panel of the truck read: G.O.D. Call 1-800-DIAL-GOD.

I got hysterical. I was laughing so loudly that I thought if anyone looked at me, they would certainly question my mental status. The "Guaranteed Overnight Delivery" truck had delivered my answer, and I began to put my energies into completing this book.

A project like this does not happen alone. It is the result of many colleagues talking together and challenging one another. It comes because people share moments of life with each other. And those life-giving moments are filled with humor, joy, and laughter. Some are even filled with tears.

Books are summaries of experiences and recorded memories of meaningful events and situations. This one is no different. Friends offered healthy, welcomed nudges. My friends are always there. They are supportive and challenging and life-giving. A special thanks to Jim Breig and Kathy Rooke for their editing help. Fireworks of thanks to Sister Roselani Enomoto, CSJ, who came from Hawaii and worked patiently and conscientiously with the manuscript. She had all the chapters spread out on the floor and arranged them in a smooth, flowing order. To Patti—who is always there for me to encourage and support me—I thank you so.

The belief and pride of my mother, Irma, and my sister, Kay, have always been a strength, encouraging me to believe that this could be a possibility. Thanks also to John Kirvan, Director of Product Development for Sorin Books, who faithfully called and offered kind words of encouragement; to Robert Hamma, Editorial Director, who set the deadlines and structure so this would be a reality; and finally to Julie Hahnenberg, Associate Editor, who edited the manuscript and was always positive and encouraging.

While I can't forget the G.O.D. truck that carried a very direct message, I believe in my God (the One not related to the truck) who graces me daily.

This book belongs to all of them. Thanks. Stay happy. Live well. Love much. Believe in yourself. And laugh often.

—Anne

1

The Ultimate Warrior and Me

There's nothing like a good laugh. It tickles our very souls. Laughter is an activity of the heart. We scrunch our souls with negativity and a lack of enthusiasm, but laughter smoothes them out. Laughter makes a noise so others can hear our feelings.

Joy is a state of mind. It really is an attitude that keeps us healthy. We are all born with a sense of humor, but it is a gift we must develop as we age. This process does not end until death. The payoff for developing a sense of humor is that we simultaneously opt for health and wellness.

That's what this book is all about. It's about joy and laughter and humor. It's about alternatives to help us live happier lives and help those around us enjoy us even more. It's about filling our hearts with life. It's about wrinkling our faces with smiles and not letting our souls dry up like prunes.

It's time we looked for smiles and joy and laughter and happiness. No one needs to look for sadness; it has a strange way of hitting us right in the face. Everyone has a horror story to tell or a crisis to relate. Maybe we get so bogged down in our tough times that we forget there is always another side we can look at. Or perhaps it's fear that no one will think we're important enough or think we need them that leads us to hold on to our heavy, sad, depressing stories.

Joy can lighten our environment. Joy frees us to breathe more easily and see things more clearly. Joy lets oxygen into our blood and into our brains. When that happens, we begin to think differently. We can be healthier, more relaxed people. The Jesuit theologian Teilhard de Chardin wrote, "Joy is the most infallible sign of the presence of God." Perhaps we can begin to see this presence of God in one another; if we did, then we would start to treat each other in a kinder, more thoughtful, more respectful way.

And it all starts with "you"—the person you look at in the mirror! Because joy is not really "doing"; it's really more like "being."

Many people have not learned the importance of taking care of themselves. We give others endless hours of our time. We begin to stutter when we have to say "no." However, if we don't take care of ourselves, we can never begin truly to pay attention to or minister to anyone else.

Recently, I was on an airplane, and as is the case for many people who travel often, I tend not to listen to the flight attendant as she instructs the passengers. The message is always the same, no matter what airline you're on. This time, however, I became distracted when I heard the flight attendant say: "And when the oxygen mask drops down, put it over your own face before you put it over the face of your child."

As she said those words, I found myself watching a mother two seats in front of me play with her little child. I began thinking about what I would do if that child were mine. I would want to protect the child and be sure the child was safe. That would be my first instinct. I would want to put the oxygen over the child's face first—and then attend to myself.

I started to picture what would happen in the jet if the scene became a reality. The cabin pressure would change so immediately that if I did not place the oxygen mask over my own face first, I would not be able to think clearly and would not have the ability to attend to the child.

Oh, the importance of taking care of ourselves! This in no way implies that we become self-centered or selfish. Rather, it means that if we do not have a respect for ourselves and a healthy sense of self-importance, then it is nearly impossible for us to develop a respect and healthy sense of importance for others.

One way to begin to take care of ourselves is to laugh. If we think about it, humor is a pretty cheap remedy. It costs nothing, and the results are fantastic. We don't need to go to a physician and seek a prescription. All we need to do is to change some negative perceptions and attitudes. And relax.

If only it were that easy! Still, we are going to use up energy one way or another, so why not make the choice that has positive payoffs?

Humor releases the same endorphins that jogging does, so we get a natural high without having to purchase new running shoes and clothing. Perhaps the most consoling piece of information is that we don't have to jar our knees or ankles or hurt any muscles or major organs to enjoy this surge of positive feeling.

Humor heals and relaxes. It renews the joy that gets hammered out of us by life's daily shocks. Humor gives us power. We often cannot control situations or events, but we can control our response. Instead of discouragement or despair, we can claim power.

The image we have of ourselves and the image others perceive are so important. How we look, how we dress, our facial expressions, how others hear our message, our eye contact—all of those create our image. Sometimes, we think, "Oh, she's in a good mood," just because the person has a smile on her face. Or we might decide, "This is not a good time to bring this item up to him," because of the expression on his face.

The examples of how we make judgments based on our observations are countless. Recently, I gave a keynote address for a Catholic School Superintendents' Day. The day began with Mass. The woman who organized the service stood behind the podium on the altar and began giving the instructions: "Please stand and greet the celebrant, and sing the opening song, 'I've Got That Joy, Joy, Joy, Joy Down in My Heart.'"

As she spoke, she stared at the group with a face that would have stopped the Energizer Bunny. I thought of how little joy was reflected in her face. It said anything but happiness to me. Yes, I judged on nonverbals. However, we must remember that so often that is our only source of information.

One time when I was on a business trip to Hawaii, everyone in the airport seemed to know this tall, good-looking, very muscular gentleman. He was surrounded by people asking for his autograph. I kept trying to find out who he was and finally decided to be direct. I said to him, "Everyone else seems to know who you are. But I don't. Who are you?" He responded, "I'm the Ultimate Warrior!" I quickly said, "I still don't know who you are!" He told me he was the World Wrestling Federation champion. I could have guessed he was a wrestler. His neck was as thick as a tree trunk! We had a lovely conversation about kids today, schools, families, and values, among other things.

The day I returned home from that trip, I spoke at a high school to almost 700 students. I began wondering how to get their attention. These students had no idea who I was or why they should stop talking to their friends to listen to someone they had never seen before. I decided that if I told them the story of the Ultimate Warrior, I would become an instant hero.

When I finished my story, one kid yelled, "You met the Ultimate Warrior?" I said, "Yes." He continued, "What did he look like?" I responded, "Just like us." Suspiciously, he said, "No, he doesn't." I said, "Yes, he does." He insisted, "No, he doesn't." I said, "Yes, he does."

Then another student yelled, "What did he sound like?" I said, "Just like us." Skeptically, he said, "No, he doesn't." I said, "Yes, he does." He maintained, "No, he doesn't." I said, "Yes, he does."

I couldn't figure out why the students doubted that I had really met the Ultimate Warrior. In fact, I was beginning to wonder if I really had. The following Sunday, I was at my mother's home for dinner. I knew that wrestling was on TV, so I began to zap through the channels to find the right program. Anyone who watches wrestling regularly would know that I didn't succeed in finding the Ultimate Warrior because each wrestler appears only once every three or four weeks. So it took me three Sundays to see the Ultimate Warrior. (I received a wonderful education during those three weeks, however. I met The Undertaker and his assistant, Pall Bearer; Tugboat; The Million Dollar Man; the Bushwhackers; and others.)

Finally, on the television screen appeared the Ultimate Warrior. No wonder the kids had questioned my description of him as looking and sounding like the rest of us. The man on the TV had paint all over his face, and he was screaming into the television: "My warriors will come and get you." That wasn't the man I had met at the airport.

I wonder how often we see others as the Ultimate Warrior, and how often others see us as the Ultimate Warrior. I met the real person at the airport; he is not the painted wrestler I saw on the screen. That one is an actor. If we stand in front of others, or if we work with some people, or if we live with someone, and if all we see is the Ultimate Warrior and never take the time to know the real person, we will never have the joy of encountering the person who is in front of us. If others see us only as the Ultimate Warrior and never get to know the true persons we are, a moment of joy (or many moments of positive energy) may be lost forever.

Check yourself in the mirror. How much war paint do you wear? Do you look like you would more eagerly hand out chokeholds than hugs?

2

New Beginnings

New Year's Day not only begins a new calendar year but also reminds us of the importance of new beginnings. The birth of a baby, a first car, the infatuation of a new relationship—all touch us with a breath of fresh air. Beginnings are always filled with a wild variety of emotions. There is always an element of excitement and surprise. The unknown contains an aspect of mystery. There is also a bit of fear and apprehension in the newness. It's like being on untested waters.

Some people make New Year's resolutions. They promise themselves that this is the year to lose weight or to exercise more or to change some piece of their lives that needs to be addressed. Of course, this is psychologically addressed with great gusto on the first day of the new year. But, ah, how that fervor disappears!

We attend to new relationships in much the same way. We call the other a million times a week and think of him or her three million times a day. We buy special cards and gifts, and include him or her in every inch of our lives. And then, not too much later, we ask, "Whatever happened to what's his (her) name?"

Perhaps all this is necessary so we can avoid ruts and deep grooves that keep us stuck. Maybe we can be comfortable with whatever we have resolved to address in our lives this year, and, if in 365 days, we can claim "success," fine. If we find, however, that our enthusiasm has not carried us through, we can also see the "success" in at least trying something new.

Beginnings have an enthusiasm that brings life and energy. They allow us to see situations with freshness and breadth. Nothing is too big to tackle. Nothing can stop us. Our visions are far-reaching and limitless. We see numerous opportunities to give our new endeavor some of our time and attention.

How about bringing a touch of newness to someone special in your life? Call someone on the phone; write a note to someone; hug someone; tell someone you love him or her.

3
Life Is a Balancing Act

We need to learn the art of caring for ourselves. It's an everyday responsibility. It involves keeping our lives in balance. It's about learning to make choices that keep us in touch with the core of who we are. It's knowing our own priorities.

There is a wonderful story about God appearing to a man in a dream. He told the man that a monk would walk past him at noontime the next day and that he would be carrying a stone. If the monk gave the man the stone, he would become the richest person in the world because the stone was a huge diamond.

When the man awoke, he couldn't wait to see if a monk would be passing by. Sure enough, at noon, a monk walked toward him and in his hand was a large satchel. The monk stopped and pulled out of the bag a diamond the size of a person's head! He told the man that he had found it in the forest. Then he gave it to the man. The man took the stone and ran home. He kept looking at it, thinking that he was the richest person in the country. But the man couldn't sleep. He kept tossing and turning all night. Finally, he got out of bed and went to find the monk, who was sleeping under a tree. He woke up the monk, gave him back the diamond, and said, "Give me the inner riches that make it possible for you to give this stone away."

Perhaps the monk has given us the secret to finding joy—real joy!

Balance is so hard to maintain in our own lives. We get busy. Demands are made of us. We have our own agendas, and we want to accomplish certain things. We drive ourselves, but sometimes we don't even know where we are going. Learning how to keep balance in our lives takes skill.

I learned what balance is from my friend Nancy, who was a Sister of St. Joseph. She was diagnosed with cancer of the hip on her fiftieth birthday. She lived only three months longer. One of the greatest gifts of my life is that during that short time I managed to visit her three or four times a week. This was no easy task since she lived in a city more than two hours away. Somehow, I managed to find routes to take me in that direction. Even when I was headed in the other direction, I found creative ways to get back there.

When I would leave Nancy, my heart would be heavy. I would feel sad and devastated and angry. I wondered how something like this could happen to someone who was so good. She was always there to be of service and to walk with others through their pain. Now, she was experiencing her own pain. As I would drive back home, I would cry and talk out loud, trying to get the sadness out of me.

One of my trips to her house is a memory I will always cherish. As I walked into Nancy's room, she said, "Hi, Annie. I'm so glad you're here. Would you pick me up and carry me into the bathroom?" Of course I would. After all, she was my friend!

After carrying her into the bathroom, cleaning her up, and freshening up her bed, I said, "Nancy, we've got to talk about this anger." Nancy quickly responded,

"Anger? What anger? I'm not angry!" Of course not. Nancy never got angry! I said to her, "Nancy, what do you mean you're not angry? You can't walk into the bathroom by yourself! You keep telling me that the sisters bring you food and say you must eat it."

That was the trigger. She said, "If they bring me one more carrot and tell me it's good for cancer. . . ." And then Nancy started talking about anger and all the things that she heroically had kept bottled up inside of her. After about two hours of this wonderful sharing I said, "You know, Nancy, we have to keep laughing! What can we do to make sure we're laughing?"

Nancy had a reply: "Stop asking me these questions and go home." I quickly responded, "Okay." But Nancy added, just as quickly, "Stop asking, but don't go home." I knew I had pushed my friend long and hard enough.

A few days later, Nancy was taken to a hospital in a city that was even farther from me. After a few weeks, we began to make preparations to bring her back to the residence where our retired or ill sisters reside. The day before bringing her home, I made one last trip. As I walked into her hospital room, there were twenty-two sisters visiting her. (There's something you need to know about sisters: When someone is in a hospital, everyone visits—whether it's sensible and appropriate or not!)

As I stood at the door of her room, Nancy smiled and said, "Annie, I'm so glad you're here." When I went over to my friend and kissed her, she whispered, "Get all these people out of here!" I whispered back, "I can't. But sit back and relax, and I'll entertain for a while."

When there were only a few people left in the room, Nancy taught me what balance is. She said, "You know, I was doing one of those Bernie Siegel exercises—the one where you walk down a long corridor and there is a door at the end of the corridor and on the other side of the door is a person with a message that you need to hear."

Now, if you knew my friend Nancy, you would have thought that she would have already figured out who would be at the other side of the door and what the message would be. But, if you've ever done one of those Bernie Siegel exercises, you know it just doesn't happen that way.

Nancy said, "I don't know what the message means. I went down the corridor, and when I got to the other side of the door, you know who was standing there? It was me. And I was seven years old, and all I was doing was laughing. I kept rolling in leaves, and I was laughing. All I did was laugh. What does it mean?" Then she reflected: "How did I learn to be so serious? How did I learn to be such an adult? Why couldn't I remember that laughing and playing were just as important as being responsible?"

I could only say, "I don't know, Nance. But do you want to spend the rest of the time we have laughing?" And we did! We had eight more days, and we spent them laughing.

None of us knows how many more days we have left. We should spend them laughing.

4
Liking Ourselves

There was a wonderful "Dennis the Menace" cartoon in the newspaper one day. He was climbing a tree with his faithful friend, Joey, close behind. Ruff was waiting on the ground under the tree, looking up at his owner. Dennis looked down to Joey on the limb below and said, "Always be proud of yourself, Joey. Sometimes, you're all you've got."

We can learn a lot from Dennis. Sometimes, we are all we've got. Yet many of us look to others for validation and affirmation. For many of us, self-esteem is defined by what others say to us or think of us. Some people can never believe they are good or even begin to believe in their own potential since they never look to themselves but only to others for this message. Sadly, there are those among us who, even when they are told they are good by others and credited for their accomplishments, still don't believe it.

Trusting ourselves is very difficult if we get into putting ourselves down and never believing in who we are. Maybe trusting ourselves comes from learning to be proud of ourselves like Dennis. Climbing a tree is an accomplishment. Learning to ride a bike, bake a pie, prepare a special meal, wallpaper a room, and even getting up in the morning on time are accomplishments. For one day, pat yourself on the back and live each deed you complete with pleasure.

5
Prescription for Joy

It's hard to study laughter and humor and joy. Mark Twain said, "Studying humor is like dissecting a frog. When you're done, you understand it, but it's dead."

I believe we already have joy and humor inside of us. When we are healthy people, we let it come out, and we share our joy with others. We may not have much control over situations and occurrences, but we do have control over how we respond to them. The power is within us. All we have to do is nurture it and believe in it.

Sometimes, we can hold on to stories and experiences to give us energy and to bring a gentle smile to our faces. We can store them inside of us—then all we have to do is learn how to recall them. Author and editor Norman Cousins taught us the value of this when he learned how to deal with a spinal disorder. When he was told that he had a one in 500 chance of getting better, he realized that much of what he was experiencing was a result of the negative stress in his life. So he mapped out a plan for himself and rented films that helped him laugh. His prescription was to put laughter in his life. He realized that ten minutes of belly laughs could get him two hours of uninterrupted sleep. And his prescription worked: he was cured. Why can't we learn from his experience?

We need to start each morning with a positive thought. I ask people to develop a very simple exercise for themselves. It can be used throughout the day, and it can produce marvelous results and tremendous highs. Here it is:

As soon as you wake up, get out of bed and *stand*. Then *breathe*. And then *smile*.

It's not hard to remember: *stand, breathe, smile*. Right after you brush your teeth, look in the mirror and repeat this simple little prescription: *stand, breathe, smile*.

Throughout the day as you start to feel some tension in your neck or in your back, *stand, breathe, smile*. It's a simple way to take care of yourself. It doesn't cost any money. Best of all, it's a conscious choice for good health.

We also need to surround ourselves with positive people. Why stay in the company of negative, complaining, unhappy people? All they do is suck our energy. Before long, we begin to feel and sound just like them. Then the world has more negative, complaining, unhappy people.

There was an old woman who lived in a dingy old hut and all she ever did was complain. Nothing was ever right, and she was always feeling sorry for herself. Her fairy godmother took pity on her one day. Waving her magic wand, she changed the dingy hut into a beautiful mansion. When the old woman walked around the mansion, she complained about its size. It took all her time to clean it. How could she ever have time for anything else? The fairy godmother, hearing her complain, again took pity on the woman and swished her magic wand over the mansion. Immediately, it was filled with servants. Now the servants could attend to the large house, leaving the woman free. But she then began to gripe about how lazy all the servants were. All of her time was spent in organizing them, checking up on them, and making sure they finished their chores. One last time, the fairy godmother took out her magic wand. She waved it over the beautiful mansion filled with servants—and it became a small dingy hut.

That old woman chose unhappiness. She got more out of being unhappy than anything else. A lot of people are like that. It's a good idea to avoid them as much as we can. There is a saying that we should take to heart: "Don't waste your time trying to befriend a mad dog."

Sometimes, we want people or things to be different. We look for nurturing from other people or from an accomplishment, and we just don't find it. If other people choose not to be there for us or if our jobs are unsatisfying, we might have to teach ourselves to walk away from them. Some things, some people, some dreams, and some plans just don't work the way we want them to. In that case, we shouldn't try to befriend those people, jobs, or dreams. We should leave them.

Hold on to healthy messages instead. Hold on to stories and experiences and peak moments that give you joy and bring laughter to your soul.

I was giving a lecture at an all-day conference for women that was sponsored by a hospital. One of the other presentations was given by a young doctor from Atlanta who presented his latest research on osteoporosis. The audience listened intently as he lectured from slides that listed the causes of osteoporosis in women. I studied the list:

"Petite." I was in no danger there!

"Vegetarian diet." Saved again!

"Exercise." Now I was beginning to like his research a lot!

I began to read ahead. Heading the second column on the slide was:

"Obesity." Okay, so now he would get me.

As he started to address the second column, he said, "Now, obesity. Oddly enough, that prevents osteoporosis."

I shouted out loud: "All right!"

Now I live with the wonderful piece of information that I won't suffer from osteoporosis. Every time I hear the word, I smile. That's what I mean about holding on to things that bring you joy and relief. They not only free us; they also empower us and allow us to be happier and more creative.

6
Loving Ourselves

"To love oneself is the beginning of a life-long romance."
—Oscar Wilde

Maybe it's a whole new idea to begin to care for and
attend to the persons we look at in the mirror. How do
we get rid of the old message that keeps running through
our heads that to think about ourselves first is selfish?
How can we learn that we have to have a level of respect
and dignity for ourselves in order to be able to give the
same respect and dignity to others?

Every time we grow into an awareness of one of our
own gifts or talents, we enrich our world and those with
whom we come into contact. We also take one more step
toward wholeness.

Perhaps if we take the time to acknowledge our good
deeds or the random acts of kindness that we do, we will
be able to smile at ourselves and remember that we are
capable and lovable.

7
Presence

An African proverb states: "Not to aid one in distress is to kill him in your heart."

How often we pass others without even realizing our ability to aid them. Aid comes in all shapes and sizes and colors and textures. We aid each other by our very presence. No presents are necessary. It is our presence that counts!

Not even words are always necessary. A gentle touch of the hand, an arm around a shoulder, the gift of listening to a need, a nonjudgmental response, lending a hand to a project, finishing a task that has already been begun by another, sitting in a hospital room with a sick person—those are the things that keep us alive in each other's hearts. They have a strange way of returning to us and filling our own hearts.

When we aid others, we give life to each other and keep each other alive. We can even experience a connection between others and ourselves. The gift gets returned.

8
Remembering

All Soul's Day, November 2, is celebrated in many countries as a day for remembering the dead and celebrating the presence of persons who have touched our lives.

I was in Peru one year for this holiday and witnessed the reverence of this custom that each generation passes down to its children. There, everyone goes to the cemetery on All Soul's Day. The custom is to hold a picnic on the gravesite of a loved one, which gives the feeling that death is really a festive occasion. The marketplace vendors cover their stalls with fresh flowers and artificial arrangements, and people purchase them to place on the graves of the deceased.

The whole family is part of this ritual. The trip to the cemetery is an all-day venture. Family members carry with them the flowers to decorate the grave as well as food—usually the favorite food of the deceased—so they may sit for hours, eating and talking with one another about the person who has died. They also bring breads ornately decorated in the shapes of animals and share them with others in the cemetery. I was given a llama and a bird, and was told this tradition is similar to our sharing valentines in the United States.

It is customary for songs to be sung, and for people to share stories about the deceased and to remember the dead with respect. In this way, the history of the deceased is passed on to the younger members of the family and teaches them to honor those who have gone before them.

How healthy for us to remember our connections with those who have touched our lives and helped us know who we are. How healthy to remember we carry these people in our thoughts and in our hearts and to respect them with the sharing of these memories.

Taking out pictures of those special people in our lives and sharing the stories of these people is another way of remembering. As Sr. James M. Barrie says, "God gave us our memories so we might have roses in December." Our memories create beautiful bouquets.

9

Perceptions

Is the glass half-empty or half-full? It's up to you.

Do you want to make this day one of your good ones, or do you want to find things that are wrong and complain about everything? It's up to you.

Listen to your thoughts. Are they mostly positive or negative?

It's up to you:

- If everything bad happens to you and nothing ever goes the way you want it to go, then maybe you need a personality adjustment.
- If you keep on thinking those negative thoughts, you'll stop liking yourself. And you should know this: no one else will like you either.
- Set out to be only positive today. If you make a mistake—too bad. If you subtract in your checkbook incorrectly—too bad. If someone doesn't like what you are doing—too bad. If you have two different socks on—too bad.

What freedom it would create to choose only positive responses.

10
Looking Outward Instead of Inward

It is a lot easier for us to see other people and decide what they are like than it is for us to look at ourselves and determine what we are like.

We look at the way others act and make judgments on their character.

We decide a lot about someone else by the choice of clothes he or she has made.

We examine items like cars and boats and material possessions, and think they give us insight into the world of somebody else.

People's jobs and positions help us determine who we think they are.

Parents often pass judgment on the families and backgrounds of their children's friends with little to go on but outward appearances.

Information gathered in these ways is rarely accurate. Many times, it is based on rumors; people spread false stories about others due to jealousy, rage, inaccurate information, personal choices, fears, selective listening, and lack of perception. Those are only a few of the reasons we know only pieces and parts of other people's worlds and personalities.

Instead of figuring out others' values or whether others are right or wrong, correct or incorrect, we should do a little personal inventory at times and spend a bit of time on self-reflection and awareness. We should look ourselves squarely in the face to judge our own actions and behaviors.

There is a story about a very successful businessman who was dating a beautiful actress. The gentleman was growing fond of her and knew he was getting close to asking her to marry him, so he hired a private investigator to find out if there was anything in her past that might prevent a successful marriage. The businessman gave the detective no details other than her name.

The report came back that her background was flawless. There wasn't a single negative thing to report. Only one questionable factor surfaced: the actress was presently dating a businessman with a questionable character!

There is a lesson for us in this story. We need to be able to see ourselves as well as we see others. Seeing ourselves does not have to be navel gazing. There is a wholesome balance in looking both out and in.

So often our observations result in black and white interpretations. We need to strive to see that gray may be a gift or a grace that allows us to relax with what is in front of us. Instead of judging everything and everyone in black and white, it would be helpful if we could begin by putting just a polka dot or two in each picture.

We need to do this with ourselves too. We need to re-learn some old things about ourselves and start to accept and respect ourselves.

11

Star Gazing

January 6—"Little Christmas"—is the day the three kings arrived at the stable, bringing gifts to the baby Jesus. It is also the feast that honors that great star that led the Magi to the Christ child.

Perhaps we should more often remember the "stars" in our lives: the people and the messages that have led us to where we are and to whom we have become.

As we look back over our lives, we remember those who have touched us with their influence and guidance. We recall situations that led us to other situations.

Some of these are not happy memories.

It is sad to remember people we have loved who are no longer in our lives because they have died or have chosen not to be part of our lives anymore.

It is sad to recall things that have not worked out as we planned.

But those messages—those stars—led us to something and perhaps provided a path that was bright enough for us to walk on. Blessings come to us in strange ways!

Perhaps as we enjoy the vast and awesome sight of our universe, we can remember the personal "stars" in our own lives and be grateful for their presence and the influence with which they touched our lives.

12

Prejudices

Dr. Martin Luther King, Jr., the courageous civil rights leader of the 1960s, organized nonviolent marches that paved the way for demonstrations for equal rights and justice.

"We have learned to swim the sea like fishes and fly the sky like birds," he once wrote, "but we have not yet learned the art of living together as brothers."

Our vision gets limited; we get goal-oriented and find ourselves ignoring each other, or not listening to each other, or not caring.

Perhaps each of us is holding on to a prejudice. It may be about race, color, gender, sexual preference, or nationality. It may be about children, animals, lawyers, bishops, co-workers. Ponder what would happen if we examined our prejudices and changed our minds.

Instead of being comfortable and maintaining stereotypes, we can teach ourselves that there are other ways of looking at and judging others and their situations. The payoff may even be that we get to see something positive in a situation or person which we had previously judged as negative.

13
Hospitality

There is a beautiful quotation in the Book of Hebrews that offers us an opportunity: "Do not neglect to show hospitality to strangers for by doing that some have entertained angels without knowing it" (Heb 13:2).

Let us live that out today so that no one lacks our hospitality:

in the way we greet another . . .

in the smiles we share . . .

in the eye contact we keep . . .

in the interest we convey by our body posture.

These are but a few gestures we can offer to show the warmth of our companionship to another.

What we can learn about ourselves as we truly listen to someone or stay open to his or her message can surprise us. How sad to think we could have missed the opportunity to have an angel touch our hearts and souls. How sad if we passed up that chance. What life-giving moments have escaped us!

Think what the world would be like if we treated everyone with this message from Hebrews in mind. It would be awesome. We would lose our prejudices and make room for differences. We would truly hear the message of the sender and eliminate all the misunderstandings in communication. We would have a warm feeling around our hearts knowing something special has happened to us.

We need to learn to look at all the people we come in contact with as angels, and give each the dignity and respect they deserve.

14

Judgments

Human beings are quick to make judgments about other people, events, actions, and behaviors.

We judge others' motives and reasons.

We put people into categories and isolate them with labels.

We decide whether we like people based on what they do, how they talk, their backgrounds, the level of their education, how they dress, and other equally superficial qualities.

What would happen if we stood in front of someone who looked very different from us (perhaps someone who frightened us) and instead of judging him or her, just stood there?

What if we stood with a stance of openness and wonder?

What if we stood with a sense of awe and surprise?

What if our agenda were to learn something rather than depend on our preconceived notions? What would happen then?

A Raisin in the Sun is a wonderful play about a black family struggling to survive not only in the world with its economic and social pressures but also within the family system itself. The grandmother, the matriarch of the family, offers some wise words to her daughter as she reprimands her for judging and belittling her brother.

The scene takes place after the son has made a bad decision regarding the family money that had been saved to buy a long-dreamed-of house. The motives of the son were good, but the outcome is devastating to the family. His sister, deeply feeling the loss, lashes out at her brother, yelling and screaming about how much she hates him. The grandmother chastises her daughter and reminds her:

> There is always something left to love. And if you ain't learned that, you ain't learned nothing. . . . Child, when do you think is the time to love somebody the most; when they done good and made things easy for everybody? Well, then, you ain't through learning—because that ain't the time at all. It's when he's at his lowest and can't believe in hisself 'cause the world done whipped him so. When you starts measuring somebody, measure him right, child, measure him right. Make sure you done taken into account what hills and valleys he come through before he got to wherever he is.

Those are powerful words, words we may want to hold in our hearts the next time someone disappoints us or chooses to act in a way we disapprove of.

And we don't have to apply those thoughts solely to those we love and are comfortable with. We can apply them to politicians, bishops, next-door neighbors, and people of different faiths. We can remember them while watching the six o'clock news and while reading the newspaper. We can recall them while waiting in line at the supermarket and finding our patience wearing thin because we have chosen the "wrong line" with people ahead of us questioning prices, using food stamps, or taking time buying lottery tickets.

I work a lot with adolescents—they are my favorite group of people. They are real. They have not permanently put on their "faces"—the adult masks we have learned to wear. Adolescents tell it like it is.

Adolescence is a stage of searching for selfhood. "Who am I?" is the question they are struggling to answer. As a result, they often try on different behaviors in an attempt to answer the question. They imitate others' actions, dress like others, and find language others understand to communicate this awkward stage. Adults have a hard time understanding some of their choices. It's even harder when the child is our own!

A few years back, I knew a terrific kid named Alex. He was thirteen and the son of a woman who had adopted him from El Salvador when he was three. She was a dedicated single parent who loved her son more than life itself. Alex's best friend, Jason, had committed suicide, and Alex became obsessed with this act. He talked only of killing himself so he could be with Jason.

Alex's mother asked me if he could come to the adolescent group that I hold each week at our counseling center. I vaguely knew him because we all belonged to the same parish, and I would often see him serve Sunday Mass. I also knew that Alex was a hyperactive child and under the care of both a psychiatrist and a psychologist. My reaction to his mother was that this group would certainly be an overload for him. She replied that he would not speak to the other two doctors, and this was her attempt to have him talk. I finally agreed to see him.

When she brought him in for the initial session, he was very nervous and avoided any eye contact with me. The session was supposed to be an information gathering session, but it was not much more than an exchange between his mother and me. At the end of the session, I asked Alex if he would agree to attend two meetings of the group; then, if he didn't like it, he needed to share that with me and we would look for alternatives. Alex agreed.

Throughout his first session, he never looked up from the floor. When asked to respond to something, he would shake his head seven times before he answered verbally.

Alex returned the second week. This time, he looked at the floor, up at someone, then back at the floor, and back up again. His verbal responses to questions came after only three shakes of his head.

Alex came back for the third session. Now I was feeling we were really making progress. This time, Alex looked around the room at the group. I jumped at this opportunity and said, "Alex, it must be terrible to lose your best friend. Do you want to talk about Jason?"

Alex said, "No, I'm not ready yet."

Believing we must respect each other's space and time, I asked him if he would do an exercise with the group. I asked if he would look at each member as they offered one positive thing about him. His only response could be, "Thank you very much." He agreed.

The group members never let me down. They all looked at Alex and said wonderful things to him about his sensitivity and ability to care so deeply. After each comment, Alex said, "Thank you very much."

That was Tuesday. Alex hanged himself on Thursday.

At the funeral Mass, his mother addressed those in attendance. She told us of her gratitude for the roles we had played in his life. Then she told stories about him. Alex was always "doing things" in school, and it was not uncommon for her to receive several phone calls regarding his behavior. She admitted the calls came with such frequency that they were no longer any cause for anxiety or panic. Then she told a story that helped me know of the depth of Alex.

One day, the teacher called to tell her that Alex had a communion wafer in his pocket. Waiting for him to come home from school, Alex's mom worked herself into a fever pitch. As he walked through the door, she screeched, "Alex, they called from school and said you have a host in your pocket. Do you?"

Alex readily admitted he did.

"Why do you have a host in your pocket?"

He replied, "I don't have anything else to give you for your birthday, Mom."

Alex knew what was important to his mother. We all learned a bit about the spirituality of a thirteen-year-old loving son, our friend Alex.

We judge. We don't know each other's stories. No one truly knows what goes on in another's world, but our judgments can create a wall that blocks us from seeing the other for who he or she really is.

15

Be "Angry Smart"

Anger can block our senses. We hear only the words that have hurt us. We hold on to memories that speak to us of disappointing events. We remember when we were passed over for a job or when a relationship ended. We recall our disappointments and failures. Recalling such things, people stop speaking to each other. We belittle others and tell family members or friends or anyone who will listen unkind things about those who are responsible for the anger.

People then begin to let anger become a part of them, but the only one who suffers from the anger is the person who holds on to it.

There are virtually no benefits in holding on to anger. It eats away only at the person who chooses to hold on to it. Some people tell every available ear their story over and over and over again. The only thing that does is rehearse the anger. There is no therapeutic value in it. It does not release the anger. It only builds a larger pot of anger and creates more of a case for one to be angry.

There isn't a person alive who has not felt anger. Anger, in itself, is not bad. No feeling has a moral judgment attached to it. It is not the feeling we are responsible for, but the behavior we choose to deal with the feeling. You can't help it if you're cold or hot. You just are. But if you choose to walk naked down a street because you are hot, you will be judged.

Anger is really a secondary feeling. It's a display of your real feelings. The next time you feel anger, stop yourself and ask what else you feel. Maybe you feel angry because you're disappointed things didn't work out as you would have liked them to. Or maybe you are angry because you are frustrated. You may have asked to have something done over and over, and it never gets done. Or maybe you feel angry because you feel so helpless and powerless. If you can begin to look at what else is under your anger, you will begin to understand the feeling.

Some people use anger to intimidate or scare others. Anger can be manipulative and destructive. Anger can grow into rage or violence. It's not uncommon to see broken bones, holes in walls, gunshot wounds, or smashed cars as results of anger that has gone out of control. Some use anger to bully or threaten others. Situations get out of control, and people can display a great insensitivity toward the victim of their anger.

Anger sometimes results in people no longer communicating with each other. There are many ways this happens:

- Some people stop communicating by no longer using words to convey their messages. They stop speaking.
- Others use blame as their mode of attack.
- Sarcasm is another way of not communicating properly; mean, hurtful statements are sent in to attack the other person.
- Instead of complaining and fighting, some people deal with their anger by "being nice." They attempt to avoid anger at all costs. These people often act hurt or tearful. This "being quiet" and "not saying anything" is frequently done so one will not "rock

the boat." It's the "peace at any price" theory. But the "nicer" these people become, the more they grow in rage, resentment, and unconscious anger. If, per chance, anger comes out, then they are ridden with guilt. Guilt is a way for them not to get in touch with their own anger because it is impossible to be both angry and guilty.

All of these methods of noncommunication are paralyzing for others, who are left helpless. Hence, it becomes impossible to come to a resolution. The healthy choice is to be in touch with what makes us angry and to look at behaviors we choose to deal with it. Some of us choose unhealthy ways to cope.

One way to view anger is to see our behaviors in one of two categories: "angry smart" or "angry dumb."

When we choose "angry smart" behaviors, we resolve the situation. We deal with the person we need to. We can move out of anger and not get stuck in the feeling. There is no need to be bitter or resentful or depressed. Some people internalize the anger, and it becomes a depression. There is a heavy price to pay for that choice; take your pick: ulcers, migraine headaches, heart attacks, colitis—to mention just a few. But "angry smart" means there is a resolution. Nothing gets buried inside of us. The anger is not left boiling and bubbling and then exploding.

"Angry dumb" means we make choices that are unhealthy for ourselves and for others. We break something or throw something or destroy something. This type of anger is destructive to all parties involved. It can involve physical acting out. But the worst part of "angry dumb" behaviors is that they eat away at people.

The destructive results of "angry dumb" behavior are not only of a physical nature. Psychologically, the price is very heavy. Voice levels are out of control. Choices of words include zingers that are hurtful and cutting. Tenderness, sensitivity, intimacy, warmth, caring, and love are absent.

Joy, laughter, and humor are hard to find when you are angry. Anger is like a brick wall, and it gets very hard to see over it, around it, or beyond it. Staying in the anger, one chooses to remain unhappy and unhealthy. To free ourselves of this and to opt for life and life-giving moments, it's important to deal with anger and what creates it for us.

Here are a few suggestions for freeing yourself of anger and opting for joy. Think of your own situation and apply these ideas to yourself. Some may fit, others may not. Some may fit today while some may be options for tomorrow.

Take a time out. Very often, we are so angry when we act that we behave irrationally. People say things they don't really mean when they're angry. Taking a few minutes of "cooling off" time is helpful. Go for a twenty-minute walk. Then reset a time to bring the situation to some conclusion.

You have the right to speak out and voice your opinion. We really fail ourselves when we do not stand up for what we believe.

Do not swallow your anger. Identify what your anger is all about. Clarify your own issues. State, as directly as possible, what you are talking about so the other person can understand it.

Talk out your anger. Name what it is you are angry about. Rehearse it, if necessary, in front of a mirror. Be clear in sending the message.

Don't use ridicule or labeling when talking about the anger. The hearer will not be able to understand your message because he or she will get caught in the label or the put-down. That only raises defensiveness. Nothing will get solved.

Blaming, preaching, moralizing, lecturing, interpreting, and diagnosing will be perceived only as put-downs. It is important not to use statements that make the hearer feel that he or she is being attacked. People don't keep their ears open when they think they are being judged.

Speak for yourself. We never have the right to speak for someone else. The use of "I" messages can help you stay on target. When a sentence begins with "I," the listener doesn't feel that a finger-pointing blame message is being sent.

Allow the other person to have his or her own feelings. Don't discount those feelings. Don't criticize the feelings, and don't tell people they have no right to their feelings.

Write out your anger. Write a letter to the person you are angry at. Tell him or her everything you want him or her to know. Just let yourself write. Spelling doesn't count. You are also free to use any language that you want. Just keep writing until you feel that you've written enough. Then read the letter. You will be surprised at what you've written. Your handwriting might even look different to you. After you have read the letter, tear it up into as many little pieces as possible and throw it away. It is very important that this step be followed. Do not save it until the next day to read again. Do not send the letter to the person to whom you have written it. The purpose of this exercise is to get the anger out of you. It will also clarify some issues for you.

Find one other person you can tell the story to. Speak as honestly as possible to this person. Tell him or her every piece of your story. However, it is very important that you choose to do this exercise with only one person. If you tell another, then another, and then another, all you have done is rehearsed your anger. That is nonproductive.

Identify the payoffs in dealing with your anger. Some people choose to hang on to the anger. They get something out of it. Figure out what that is.

Go out and do some physical activity. Go for a walk or jog, or shoot some baskets. Find a pond and throw some stones. Cut the grass. Shovel some snow. Go swimming. Play golf.

Listen. If the anger is from the other person toward you, then you need to listen to what he or she is saying. Don't interrupt. Try to hear the message as objectively as possible. Allow them to have their own opinions.

Watch your tone of voice. Yelling only produces yelling. Screaming blocks ears. Repeating what you need to say as briefly as possible in a tone of voice that is as soft as you can manage makes it more likely that the other person will listen and really hear what has been said.

16
No Need to Be Perfect

I want to remember positive things about myself, and I want to start to love myself and what I am and what I do. That means I have to remember that while I still have some rough edges, they don't make me bad.

Human beings aren't perfect. And that's all I am—a human being. So why do I expect more of myself than of others? I need to remember that human beings trip and fall, sometimes say things they don't mean, and make mistakes. Those are not really failures. They are ruts and grooves that we need to grow into an awareness of. Then we see them as they are, not as utter failures or weaknesses in our personalities but as things that human beings need to attend to and be aware of so that we may also allow others to be that human in their own lives.

Loving ourselves means loving even our rough edges. That doesn't mean we never address these issues or behaviors, but that we see them for what they are—traits of being human.

Why do we always think we have to be perfect? You know—never make mistakes, always say the right things, never step out of line, etc.? What an injustice we do to ourselves. We keep ourselves so locked into boundaries that we often miss opportunities to discover new options. We are so rigid with ourselves that we never give ourselves any breathing space. If only we can relax and breathe easier, we will find spontaneity and creativity. Our perceptual world will broaden and we will discover new ways of doing things and hearing things.

Isn't it strange that so many of the great things that are accomplished are the results of mistakes or numerous persistent attempts? Babe Ruth struck out 1,330 times in his baseball career. He never would have been able to set some fifty baseball records if he had concentrated on his outs instead of his hits.

How often we focus on what we have not accomplished instead of what we have accomplished. We can hear a hundred positive statements and a single negative one, and yet dwell on that one negative remark. Years later it's the only one we remember!

Being perfect is a tough ideal. Never to deviate from that goal of perfection contributes to unhealthy expectations and even physical sickness. Why are we so hard on ourselves? Do we think it is virtuous? Why is it better for us to put ourselves down, negate our good works, discount our achievements and accomplishments? Why are we so quick to hold on to mistakes and accent our own foibles?

We are not bad. As a matter of fact, we are good! We know that God didn't create junk. We need to acknowledge our strengths and rejoice in our achievements and accomplishments. If we care about ourselves, we must nurture our gifts and nourish our own spirits. Without accepting the "good side" of ourselves, we can never attain wholeness. We can never be complete.

We are gifted people.

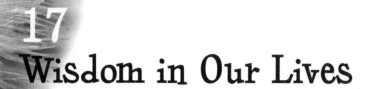

17
Wisdom in Our Lives

"Joy is wisdom, time an endless song," said poet William Butler Yeats.

Wisdom is like:

- having every part of us alive and awake;
- having every part of us work as one so that a complete picture is presented;
- having an awareness of our hearts, minds, bodies.

It's like coming alive. It's seeing, hearing, tasting, touching, feeling, perceiving, and dreaming. It's being compassionate and caring and intelligent. It's being whole.

Most of the time, we do not allow ourselves the luxury of being so in touch with every moment that we feel the joy and wisdom that is present. To be a wise person is to be able to see beyond the moment in front of us and breathe into the next. It doesn't hold us captive. Rather, it is a mind-blowing experience that takes us to creative awareness.

All of us who have ever had the privilege of knowing a wise old person (and it has nothing to do with chronological age) know what the experience is like. We sit in awe of their profound wisdom. It's not conveyed to us by a lot of words—the message comes through the person.

Not too long ago, my little friend Amanda was dealing with the loss of her best friend, Barbara. They had been inseparable, and their very presence always touched my heart. Amanda didn't really understand this thing called death and was filled with questions about heaven, where Barbara was, spirits, where one's body goes, and what happens then. She asked me a wonderful question one day in her search for some information.

"Anne, everyone is talking about Barbara being up there. Well, if she is up, what is down?"

That led us into a long, detailed conversation about heaven and hell, and what we both thought they were all about.

"Well, what's the other place?" she asked.

"What other place?"

"You know, purr-ger-tory."

"Oh, purgatory! [I was aware I was speaking to an eight-year-old child. However, she had her questions lined up, and I was struggling to respond to her satisfaction.] Well, some people believe that when a person dies and that person isn't ready to go to heaven, then that person waits in purgatory until they are ready to go to heaven."

"Oh, Anne," Amanda responded, "Barbara is not in purr-ger-tory. And we won't go to purr-ger-tory. We've all waited long enough."

Ah! The wisdom of an eight-year-old. She cut right through the words and applied their meaning to her understanding. Amanda truly knew her friend. She knew of the waiting, the suffering, and the long, weary, unexplained moments they had both lived. Yes, there was no need to wait any longer. Her friend had waited long enough, and her friend was in heaven. How could anyone ever question that?

Wisdom has many faces. It knows no age, gender, educational level, or religion. But once that wisdom touches you, you truly know joy. It expands your heart and changes your thoughts. *You* change.

18
Hugs

Touching is probably one of the most important gifts we give to each other. If a baby is not held, it dies.

We never lose the need to have someone put an arm around us or take hold of our hands. We all need the human touch; otherwise, we shrivel up and die.

But isn't it strange that the thing we all need so much is so often the one thing that we are afraid of?

I received a piece of mail that contained only a quotation about hugging. The author is unknown, but the words are powerful.

Hugging

Hugging is healthy.
It helps the body's immune system which keeps you healthier.
It cures depression, reduces stress, and induces sleep.
It is invigorating, rejuvenating, and it has no unpleasant side effects.
Hugging is nothing less than a miracle drug.
Hugging is practically perfect: There are no moving parts, no batteries to wear out, no periodic checkups. It is low-energy consumption, high-energy yield, inflation-proof, non-fattening, with no monthly payments, no insurance requirements, theft-proof, non-taxable, non-polluting and, of course, fully returnable!

What more can be said? It feels good to get a hug. It communicates volumes. Wouldn't it be wonderful if we made a vow to hug ten times a day? I'll bet there would be a lot more smiles around. Little kids don't seem to have a problem getting their quota of hugs. How about you?

19

When Things Are Not the Way You Want Them

I have a wonderful little girl in my life who always brings me joy and happiness. She helps me keep things in perspective. Children have a way of gracing our lives with reality and balance.

Lesley was born with an abundant supply of self-esteem. Truly, she has more than an average person needs to get through life successfully. She seems to go merrily to each new task and to bring to it a new supply of energy and enthusiasm. Fear is not part of her vocabulary or thought process. She is always eager to learn something new, and her every task becomes a new experience that makes life a bit fuller.

Lesley's brother Stephen is not blessed with the same degree of self-esteem. He questions himself a lot more, is a bit more hesitant to try new things, and wonders about the outcome of a projected task before he even begins it. Stephen, however, is a gifted saxophone player who could challenge many mature and trained musicians. Yet, when he was asked to play his sax in a Christmas play for the high school, Stephen, who was only eight, did not view this request as an honor. To him, it was a scary and terrifying task.

He was out in the car with my sister, who is his god-mother, and Lesley. Stephen began questioning my sister: "What if I make a mistake during the concert?"

My sister assured him immediately, "Stephen, you will be fine. Don't worry about a thing."

Stephen continued, "But what if I make a mistake?"

My sister quickly responded, "It doesn't matter, Stephen. We are all so proud of you. Don't worry about it."

Stephen said a bit louder, "Yeah, but what if I make a mistake?"

Lesley was in the back seat of the car, listening to her eight-year-old brother. Even though she was only four, she never questioned whether she had the right to get involved in this intimate conversation.

"Stephen," the voice from the back seat began, "do you remember when I was in the ballet recital? What happened? I fell down right in the middle of it. And what did I do, Stephen? I picked myself up and started all over again. Now, Stephen, just pick yourself up and start all over again."

The wise solution was evident to a four-year-old who was gifted with the confidence not to get stuck in a mistake or failure. She didn't even get stuck in the event. Somehow, she just picked herself up and started all over again. No mess! No hesitation! No doubting! No wondering about what others were thinking!

Sometimes, we all need to have a Lesley in the back seat. We need to hear, "Just pick yourself up and start all over again."

Easy? No way! But the energy and freedom lie in picking ourselves up and starting all over.

20
Expectations

Let's call today Choose to Be Happy Day!

That would help us remember three things:

1. Happiness is a choice.
2. Not all people choose to be happy.
3. It takes practice for some people to learn #1.

Do you think that some people are born to be happy while others are not? That's like believing that some people are born good and others are created evil. Do you believe it is another person's fault that you are not happy? It isn't. That's why we need a day to remind ourselves that our happiness is *our* happiness; and happiness doesn't come from someone else or because of someone else.

It is certainly true that we live within a network of people who influence us, a network that includes our family, friends, colleagues, people with whom we worship, and our neighbors. We have expectations for all of them and they have expectations for us. Sometimes, those expectations are rational and consistent. At other times, they are irrational or contradictory.

When we become disappointed or upset with ourselves or others, it is usually because our expectations are not met. Sometimes, we must rethink and change those expectations. To hold on to an unreasonable expectation only keeps us hurt, angry, and unhappy.

21

Lines That Are Curved

Smiles are the curve lines on our faces that always enhance our appearance and give hope to those who see us. Smiling, like laughter, is contagious. It creates a mirror effect—smile and we get back a smile. As Phyllis Diller says, "A smile is a curve that sets everything straight."

It pays to smile. Waitresses report bigger tips when they smile at customers. Patients in hospitals feel that a smiling nurse helps them heal more quickly than an unsmiling nurse. Even some thieves who have held up convenience stores have divulged that they did not rob clerks who greeted them with smiles.

It has been proven that when we are smiling we are triggering less serious memories within our own bodies. According to a study done by psychologist James Laird of Clark University, facial expressions can trigger our moods by returning us to memories. Laird found that students remembered happier thoughts when they were smiling. Conversely, he found that grim stories were more easily remembered when students were frowning. And it does not matter if we are really smiling or faking it. A phony smile can trigger happy thoughts just as easily as a genuine one.

Dr. John Diamond in his book *Your Body Doesn't Lie* states that smiling helps strengthen the thymus gland, an important contributor to a healthy immune system, because the zygomaticus major muscles (smile muscles) and the thymus gland are closely linked.

Dr. David Bresler, a former director of the pain control unit at the University of California in Los Angeles, looked at the benefits of using the zygomaticus major muscles. His research showed that smiling can help us take the first half-step away from physical and psychological pain. It is only a part of an overall picture, but when we can smile in spite of our pain, we can focus less on our discomforts. A smile can set things straight.

22
Others Sometimes Tell Us Who We Are

Many people never take the time to learn who they are. They live off the messages of those who tell them that they are good or not good, that they can achieve certain things or that they have failed.

Some spend a lifetime as strangers to themselves. To be happy, whole persons, we must be free enough:

- to know ourselves,
- to look in a mirror and choose to like what we see,
- to own our strengths and our weaknesses,
- to attend to our needs, and to nourish our bodies and minds,
- to hear what others say about us.

Jean-Paul Sartre claimed, "Freedom is what you do with what has been given to you." Eleanor Roosevelt reminded us: "No one can make you feel inferior without your consent." Why would we give that much power to anyone else? Why do we give charge of ourselves to others?

It is essential to our happiness that we respect and accept ourselves. That doesn't mean we won't have a few things about ourselves that are not perfect and that we won't like. It does mean, however, that we have a sense of integrity and self-worth.

There is a benefit in listening to others and hearing what they are saying about us. We cannot truly know and accept who we are unless others take the time to tell us. We need others in our lives, and we need others to affirm us. It validates us. Without affirmation, we will never be able to know ourselves.

Still, many of us hear only the negative things that are said or remember only the rejections. People hold on to those messages for years without choosing to listen to them or deciding what to do with them. Some just need to be discarded. Others need to be heard to provide us feedback so that we may make appropriate changes in our lives.

23
Labels Define Us

Have you ever noticed that we often speak in sentences that don't use a universal vocabulary?

Everything today has been reduced to symbols, to labels. We begin to refer to ourselves and others using those labels, and they form a message system that is loaded with judgments and interpretations which may or may not be accurate. For example, it is not uncommon to hear talk of AA (Alcoholics Anonymous), ACOA (Adult Children of Alcoholics), and OA (Overeaters Anonymous); a number on the Enneagram; and words like "dysfunctional" and "co-dependent." They are commonly used in both professional environments and in casual conversation at cocktail parties.

For some people, such labels become a status symbol. People begin to define and think of themselves in terms of the initials. There is a whole set of initials for academe: B.S., B.A., M.S., M.A., Ph.D. Some labels indicate professions: lawyer, doctor, teacher, priest, sister, accountant, banker, author, humorist, commentator, meteorologist. There are other labels as well: divorced, widowed, single-parent, blended-parent family, step-parent family, lesbian, gay.

We also have labels for racial and ethnic categories: African American, Caucasian, Hispanic, and Native American. And, of course, we have traditional roles that have been labeled: mother, father, brother, sister, grand-parent, aunt, uncle, cousin. The list goes on and on.

We must not get caught in labels. Labels are like houses—we often see only the exterior. Hence, our information of what is inside is very limited. Not until we are allowed into a home can we understand what it's all about. We can get to know the identity of the house by the number of rooms, the style of the wallpaper, the paint colors, the pictures on the wall, the furniture. All of that is a mystery until we are inside.

People are like that. We see them so differently once we know them. We learn personality traits and interests. We learn what they like and dislike and how they enjoy spending their free time. They become personal to us and are no longer described in physical terms or by labels.

Often, our awareness changes as we get to know another person better. First impressions are frequently incorrect. Labels do not identify who this person really is. If we view someone as an ACOA, we may be quick to judge that he or she will be afraid of intimacy and will be aloof. If we judge one to be co-dependent, we may mis-judge a friendship or support system. The fault is in the label.

Labels have a way of keeping us stuck in the past. And although yesterdays certainly will always influence us, if yesterdays control us, we will never be free. Labels can create un-freedoms.

24

Take a Risk

Sometimes, we don't experience happiness in our lives because we don't risk enough to find it. We do the same things over and over again. We confine ourselves to activities that we think might make us happy. We repeat the same old things year after year and feel safe and comfortable. But we never re-examine our activities or try something new, or create a new hobby or relationship or pattern in our lives that brings excitement. So boredom and complacency become characteristic of our lives. They are really enemies of happiness.

Take the opportunity to do something out of your normal routine:

- Greet a stranger with a compliment.
- Invite a person to whom you don't owe anything to dinner.
- Drive to work a different way.
- Call a person you know would love to hear from you.
- Jot a note to a lonely person or to someone who lives alone.
- Wear something to work that you have never worn before.
- Spend half the day at a museum.
- Go for a drive to a place that you have never been before.

When we do something that expands our comfort zone and experience the pleasure that comes from opening ourselves to a new experience, we open our world to risks, surprises, and new energy.

25
Lighten Up

Spontaneity can be a gift, but rigidity often destroys the spontaneity in our lives. For us to be healthy people, we need to risk living in the moment. It is not necessary to plan every second of our lives. And even if we do, we must be willing to be surprised at those plans and how they often take on new shape.

Humor can never be in our lives if we are not free enough to risk living in the moment. Mae West once said, "Whenever I have to choose between two evils, I always like to try the one I haven't tried before." Risk, spontaneity, and creativity may not be so different from each other!

Humor has the ability to turn things around. Difficult situations are not dead end streets. There is a wonderful story from the Yiddish tradition that illustrates this point.

There once was a rabbi with such a golden voice that everybody ran to hear him. In every city he visited, women showered him with flowers and merchants showered him with gifts.

One day the rabbi's faithful sleigh driver said, "Rabbi, for once I'd like to be the one receiving all the honors and attention. Just for tonight," the driver suggested, "change clothes with me. You be the driver and I'll be the rabbi."

The rabbi agreed but added, "Remember, clothes do not make the man. If you're asked to explain some difficult passage of the Talmud, see that you don't make a fool of yourself."

So the driver changed clothes with the rabbi and the rabbi became the driver. When the two men arrived at the next town, the bogus rabbi was received with much enthusiasm and he enjoyed it immensely. Since he had heard the real rabbi's speech hundreds of times, he delivered it perfectly. Then the dreaded question-and-answer period came. An aged scholar arose and asked a rather difficult and tricky question. The real rabbi in the back of the room thought, "Now he'll make a fool of himself."

But the driver managed to turn the situation around. "A fine scholar you are! Why, your question is such a simple one that even the old uneducated fellow who drives my sleigh must know the solution. Driver, come up here to the platform and answer this poor fellow!"

Ah! To be creative and free to come up with a solution. It is within all of us to be able to do just that. However, if we hold on to things the way they are supposed to be, then we can never relax enough to see other options.

As we read in Proverbs, "Where there is no vision, the people perish" (29:18). Vision implies spontaneity, surprise, creativity, and wonder.

26
Success

We place too much emphasis on succeeding. We use success to measure who we are and what our worth is and how much we are liked and respected.

We measure ourselves by how much we get done. How sad!

Did you ever look at a parent eyeing a report card? The first thing they look at and comment on are the marks. How high are they? Why aren't they higher?

Employers judge their employees on how much gets accomplished and produced. Often, words of praise are not heard, but hardly a flaw goes by unnoticed.

We even judge God on how much gets accomplished and how many prayers are answered and if things are going the way we want them to go.

Confucius stated: "In all things, success depends on previous preparation; and without such preparation, there is sure to be failure." I guess that means that we have to work toward success and that we need to be responsible all along the journey toward accomplishment. We need not judge ourselves along the way since we are walking toward the accomplishment. Each step will define the story. Each word of the story is written by us.

It is important to be aware of our own successes. We all need a pat on the back, and sometimes we have to pat ourselves. This is true humility. When we are free enough to acknowledge our accomplishments and successes, we are really humble. We are also being responsible, since these gifts and accomplishments are a part of us.

27
Love Benefits

"Love" is a strange word. We use it in regard to everything. We love people and animals and food and flowers. Everyone is looking and searching for love. Love makes people act differently. Sometimes, love even causes tears. Love eases burdens. Love feels good. Love songs are written so this strange feeling can be expressed with both words and music.

We hear that love makes the world go round and that love means you never have to say you're sorry. When lovers are together, they find reasons not to leave each other. Gifts are purchased to say "I love you."

Now we are finding out that true love (is there any other?) can aid the immune system. It promotes healing and extends one's life span. *Longevity* magazine reported the phenomenon of true love being beneficial to both the lover and the one loved: "One key to love's medicinal power may be the lover's high, the euphoric state produced when amphetamine-like substances called phenythethylamines are released in the brain during the excitement phase of falling in love."

It also reported that a 1992 Ohio State University College of Medicine study found that couples who acted less loving toward each other had decreased levels of disease-fighting antibodies and T-cells. A decrease of antibodies and T-cells can cause illness and helplessness, and even death.

Recently, *Life* magazine reported about twin girls, Kyrie and Brielle Jackson, who had been born twelve weeks early. They immediately were placed in separate incubators. Kyrie, who weighed two pounds, three ounces, slept very peacefully. Brielle, the smaller twin, had breathing and heart-rate problems. She did not gain any weight and fussed when anyone tried to comfort her.

Then a nurse tried a technique called double bedding and put the sisters together for the first time since they had shared the womb. Brielle snuggled up to Kyrie and calmed right down. With her sister near, Brielle began to thrive.

Ah! The power of touch.

Why are we so afraid of loving and trusting? We build walls around our hearts and protect ourselves from the very passion we are yearning for. We choose to die instead of living with the strength that the power of physical touch gives to us.

28
Oh Joy!

Here's what I know about joy:

- We cannot hold on to joy. It is not a possession we clutch in our hands. We can't grab it or capture it. We can't make a choice never to let go of it.
- It would be foolish to believe we can experience joy every single waking moment of our lives.
- Joy truly comes when we are living and experiencing the present moment, and are in touch with that awareness. It implies being open and loving and aware of ourselves. *self aware* *connected*
- Joy also implies that we have a sense of connection. We are not isolated people, and we cannot imprison ourselves.
- Joy expands our world to include all the goodness around us. We see beauty in flowers, in trees, in plants and animals, in stars and clouds, in works of art, in the faces of young children, and in the old.
- Joy fills the emptiness of *my* our lives and touches us *me w/* with a reality of hope and life-energy. It's a shot in the arm. Joy is the push into the next moment of life that opens us to the grace of the moment.
- With joy in our lives, we begin to see things differently. We see mistakes as an opportunity to learn. We perceive blocks in our path of life as stepping stones rather than stumbling blocks. We learn to view awkward moments as possibilities.

29
Focus

Little children have not learned the art of blocking out others with their judgments and negativity. They only know how to live this very moment and play. When a moment is over, they move on.

We should re-learn the art of playing from children and recognize the endless energy present in their bodies. They can teach us how to set priorities and show us that everything is not work and responsibility. They will open our eyes to newness and life, give us the ability to laugh and giggle and trip and make mistakes. They possess the gift of attentiveness and also the gift of ignoring that which is not important or that which does not hold their interest.

Little children are free enough to cuddle on our laps and persistent enough to nag us into doing what they would like to do. It is in the eyes of a child that we can see our God and that we are made aware of the awesomeness of life.

30
Play—And Then Play Some More

We've all heard the saying: All work and no play makes Jack a dull boy. Why is it that we put restrictions on play so that we have to earn it? We were told as children that we couldn't go out to play unless our homework was done. We had to eat our vegetables or there would be no dessert. All chores had to be done before we could go to the movies.

Is that how we learned that play comes second to responsibility? Is that how we have learned to be so serious rather than learning how to play for the sake of playing? Some believe that play is a waste of time. If all work and no play makes Jack a dull boy, does that mean dull is what we want to be?

Dullness leads to boredom, and one then lacks spontaneity and energy. We cut off our creativity and become robots. We need to play more to be alive. In reality, we accomplish more work when we have time to play.

31
Surround Yourself With Laughter

People who help us laugh are truly gifts to us. They give us energy and help us stay balanced. They help us keep things in perspective and remind us that we do not have to be perfect. They teach us acceptance of self and others. They empower us with the hope and belief that negativity can rob us of. Discouragement diminishes. Depression lifts. Smiles appear. Risks are taken.

An article I read recently described the tragic accident that paralyzed actor Christopher Reeve. Here was a strong, strikingly muscular, active man. An expert horseman, he was nevertheless thrown from his mount and is now in a wheelchair, paralyzed from the neck down.

After the initial ordeal, he told of a friend's visit that changed his attitude and gave him life. Reeve was extremely depressed when comedian Robin Williams appeared in his hospital room dressed outlandishly as a Russian doctor. Reeve admitted that this was the first time he had laughed since the accident. He added that it was at that moment he knew he was going to be all right. The gifts of friendship, caring, and laughter gave him hope and inspired him.

When we laugh, we keep our hopes alive. We empower ourselves to believe that change can happen, that things can get better, that, at least, all is not hopeless. Laughter does not erase pain; it gives us the ability to handle pain.

Sorrow, pain, suffering, and loss are all part of life. In Proverbs 14:13, we read, "Even in laughter, the heart is sorrowful." Sometimes, we have a mistaken notion that laughter implies everything is wonderful and perfect, but laughter is more like putting on a pair of sunglasses. It doesn't cancel the sun; it just allows people to be more comfortable and relax their eyes so they can see more clearly.

It is important that we put in our lives people who can be sunglasses for us and people who possess the same gifts Robin Williams has. Some of us may claim we do not know anyone who can tickle our hearts with joy, but in reality they are there. And when we open ourselves to that awareness, we begin to see we have lots of these gifts in our lives.

32
The 70-mph Explosion

What happens to us that robs us of our sense of humor? What drains us so that we are willing to let go of such a life-giving grace?

Research indicates that an infant laughs when he or she is ten weeks old. At sixteen weeks, an infant laughs almost every hour. When a child is four years old, he or she laughs every four minutes unless we interfere with the child experiencing happiness!

It's a fact: When we laugh more and when we have a sense of humor, we are more creative thinkers and healthier people.

A good laugh releases mental and physical tension in our bodies.

Our whole body benefits when we laugh. Our temperature goes up at least one degree. The larynx and glottis begin to rock. Air rises along the windpipe and bangs against the trachea. Laughter then explodes out of our bodies at almost seventy miles per hour. For all those people who are worried about getting old and slowing down, remember that we can do something at seventy miles per hour all our lives!

Laughter keeps us open to the possibilities and options that are available. So often we let our attitudes or anxieties lead us to the point of not being able to see the whole picture. We get stuck in our own stuckness. We walk around with blinders on, seeing only from a narrow point of view. As a result, everything gets heavy and black and bleak. Sadness and depression may overcome us.

What a wonderful gift when someone can free us from the feelings that weigh us down and help us learn to laugh, smile, and see some healthy options. It's happened to all of us: We are in a situation where the tension is so thick that you can hardly breathe. Then someone says something, and everyone laughs. You know how it feels. Your body relaxes, and the tension in your neck and back goes away.

Humor helps us to see through things. It offers us bifocals even when we don't think we need to wear glasses. It keeps things in perspective.

So often what blocks us from seeing and experiencing humor and joy is our attitude. We hold on to negative thoughts and memories, and they become the driving forces that determine our beliefs and thoughts and actions.

One bad experience, one rejection, one significant loss, one person saying something bad about us, someone not liking something we've done, not receiving the approval of a co-worker or friend—incidents like these become obsessions, and we measure everything by them. They also become our un-freedoms, our controllers, choking any joy we might have.

Sometimes, it takes work to be able to see the joy and humor that exist right in front of us. Anthony DeMello told a wonderful story about a man who wanted desperately to win the lottery. He prayed, "Dear God, please let me win the lottery!" The next week, he prayed louder, "Dear God, please let me win the lottery. My family will be taken care of." Each week, he prayed a bit louder. Finally, about six months later, he was on his knees with his hands folded tightly, shouting, "Please God, let me win the lottery. My family needs so many things. Then they will be taken care of."

From heaven, he heard a booming voice: "It would be helpful if you bought a ticket."

That's what it's all about. We have to buy lottery tickets! We can't just assume that humor or joy will hit us in the face. We have to start to look for it the way a gold prospector looks for nuggets.

It's also important to address our own perceptions and attitudes. So many of us hold on to negative thoughts without even being aware of what those thoughts are doing to us. They act as shut-off valves in our lives, cutting off all life-giving thoughts, making us emotionally comatose.

Since negative thinking clogs the brain, it is obvious that positive thinking unclogs it, allowing creativity and options to flow freely. We begin to find ourselves energized. Our stress level decreases, and our attitudes begin to be positive.

We must become aware of our perceptions, and of the fears and biases that shape those perceptions. Our own desires and wishes, at times, determine what we see (or want to see).

Perhaps you have heard of the farmer who had only one dream: for his two sons to inherit the farm and to love it as much as he did. For one of his sons, that might happen, but the other wasn't sure. Daily, that son searched for an answer as to what he would do with his life. Should he stay and be a farmer, or should he go off and get involved in another line of work? One day, he ran across the farm, calling out to his father.

As he approached his father, he hurriedly told him that he had to leave the farm to go and preach Christ.

The father was rather puzzled at this announcement and asked how his son had reached his decision. The son said, "Oh, it was really easy. I was looking up at the clouds and I saw two letters 'P.C.' That means 'Preach Christ.'" The father looked at his son and asked, "What makes you think it doesn't mean Pick Corn?"

We are all like the farmer's son at times. We want something to be a certain way, so we put blinders on and limit our vision. The worst part is that some of us become so convinced we are right that we close our minds and seal our ears to any other alternatives. But humor and joy open our minds, ears, and eyes to new possibilities and opportunities.

33

Laugh Often

Laughter tickles and brings life to our souls. When we laugh with others, we form a bond with them and grow closer. Laughter energizes our whole body, and the effects of laughter can stay with us for at least forty-five minutes.

Doesn't it make sense to choose something that gives us life and energy? It doesn't cost any money, and we don't have to buy any special clothes or join a club. To find laughter in the present moment requires only our desire to find it. Laughter is ever-present. But if we have blinders on, we limit our vision and cannot find the gift of joy that is there.

There is a story about a minister who is standing over the bed of a dying man shouting, "Renounce Satan; renounce Satan and be forgiven!" The dying man opens one eye, looks at the minister, and says, "Sure, easy for you to say, Father, but in my situation I don't dare alienate anybody."

We interpret what is going on subjectively. What is happening in our lives and what we are carrying in our hearts determines what we burden our bodies with. Each moment begins to be reprioritized and we gain control of our lives.

When we must deal with a crisis or when a sickness invades our bodies or when a loss changes our lives, we confront our own values and what is important to us. This is exactly what happened in a cancer survivors group I have had the wonderful opportunity of interacting with. These men and women are different people today because of the cancer that changed their bodies and hearts and minds. They put things in different order, and things that at one time were so important to them now hold little value. They redefine how and with whom they spend their time. The disease has given them all a new lease on life and that lease has opened up doors they may never have seen or chosen to enter. They worry differently and spend less time on unimportant things. They have learned to let go of burdens carried in their hearts that contributed to stress, and, admittedly, they have learned to laugh more. Laughter has become as much a part of their day as oxygen.

Laughter reminds us to keep what is important in front of us and not be distracted by clutter. The energy of laughter relaxes our bodies and opens our pores so that positive energy can bless our existence.

34
Free Your Spirit

Maybe we should all rent a four-year-old for the weekend. That child would teach us perspective, wisdom, and balance. We would learn that we need to wake up parts of us and become alive. We could truly learn how to live.

Many adults do not know how to use their heads, hearts, bodies, and souls. We're always trying to separate pieces of who we are. Some of us never learned to see and hear and touch and taste and smell and dream and dance and laugh. These people live by shoulds and should-nots and always and never, and become rigid in their ways.

Age has nothing to do with it. You can become old as a very young child. Or you can chose to be a childlike old person. One is free and alive; the other has died. You don't have to be dead to die. There are a lot of people walking around who are not dead but have not yet learned how to live. They postpone and wait. It's never the right time. They never have what they need. Life is full of limitations and restrictions for such people. Unfortunately, they stop growing and decide to survive rather than to live.

Some people look for instant relief. Television tells us that pills do it quickly for us. There is an instant remedy for every ailment or pain. No need to suffer any inconvenience at all. So waiting and patience are not understood.

Laughter does not come easily in our world:

- Corruption exists in the business world, sports arena, and government agencies.
- Crime rates in the United States seem always to be rising, and we live in fear of becoming a statistic of burglary, mugging, assault, or robbery.
- Alcohol abuse accounts for thousands of homicides, domestic disputes, and traffic fatalities.
- Child abuse and partner abuse statistics are astounding.
- Teen pregnancy continues to be a major concern.
- Nearly half of American marriages end in divorce.
- Unemployment is too high.
- More than thirty-two percent of Americans are poor.

So what is there to laugh about? Laughter is almost sacred. It's a spontaneous reflection that indicates freedom. Laughter discloses true joy, beauty, and affirmation. It is the power to see through moments of humanness and despair. It is the ability to be free enough to know there is a balance and all can be well.

Some people wait for others to make them happy. Some let others set the mood and attitude of their work area. Some let others determine the whens, hows, whys, and ifs of their lives. For us to be whole and happy people, we need to own ourselves. All of us need to have a life!

If you are waiting for your friend or partner to go to a movie and she doesn't want to go, go alone or ask someone else to go with you. If you are waiting for a person to go to a concert and he doesn't want to go, find someone else. Our lives depend on our choices. We can spend a lot of time waiting for someone else to meet our needs or we can find another way to have our needs met.

Life is worth living! It's important to live our lives. Waiting for others to decide to do things with us risks our never doing anything at all.

35
Laughter:
The Soul's Medicine

Laughter is a gift and a blessing. It bonds us together, it connects us, and it creates a sense of belonging. Laughter also heals. We can bring its joy and energy into our bodies, relax our muscles, decrease our anxiety, and send some oxygen up to our brains, which will help us get a healthy perspective. Laughter is really a gift we give ourselves. When we laugh, negativity disappears. We are able to relax enough to see new options and ways of looking at things.

Laughter doesn't let us get stuck in ruts or in negative thinking. Laughter is like putting on a new pair of glasses: we see more clearly and become aware of details and things not in our old vision. A beautiful Zen poem says, "Since my house burned down, I now have a better view of the rising moon." Ah! How our perspective changes!

What freedom becomes ours when we laugh! We open doors of belief for ourselves. Laughter gives us the courage to trust ourselves so we can try something even if we can't do it well; or, we can attempt to learn something and not fear failure.

Four-year-old children laugh 400 times a day, adults only 15 times a day. Maybe we should hang around with four-year-olds. They will help us keep things in perspective. They can teach us how to laugh—you know, the real belly-laughs! And perhaps that is the real meaning of the gospel passage: "Unless you become like little children you cannot enter the Kingdom of Heaven."

But laughter is like a vacation. If we don't plan it, it doesn't happen. We have to care enough about ourselves that we put laughter into our lives every day. We need to surround ourselves with people who help us laugh, stories that energize us, moments that allow us to feel lighter and breathe easier. Studies show us that most of our free time comes not in grand get-a-ways but rather in scraps of time. We gain days of opportunity three minutes at a time (a cup of coffee, a moment of sharing with a colleague, a hug, a three-minute phone call). We have to plan these three-minute energizers and put them in our daily schedule. These are the blessings of our day for us. These are the grace-filled seconds that give us the strength to deal with the heavy things of our day. These are the moments that keep us in touch with reality. It is these moments of laughter that create the positive attitude we all need, that offer health to us and provide the food we need for our souls. Yes, laughter is soul food!

The benefits of laughter are numerous. We can become more open, healthy, and creative people by keeping laughter in our lives.

We exercise our organs when we laugh. (It sure beats jogging!) We create community and feel bonded with people with whom we laugh. We tend to share more with these people and are more comfortable in their presence.

Laughter has to become as important as eating and breathing. Just as we need food to keep our bodies alive, we need laughter to keep our hearts healthy and our souls vibrant. When we can laugh, we tend to see options that are available to us that get blocked and distorted when we don't laugh. It is this visible laughter that helps us enrich our sense of humor.

Humor is a grace. It lets us work more effectively and play more enthusiastically. Humor teaches us to be creatively flexible. It is a way of seeing ourselves and others, a way of dealing with serious issues in our lives.

Laughter doesn't mean we do not deal with difficulties or never feel hurt or sadness or never cry. Far from it! When we have this sense of humor, we are free enough to be able to feel the sorrow that leads to tears.

Laughter gives us the ability to deal with what might otherwise terrify us. It lets us face the fears that could suffocate us. Laughter really diminishes physical and psychological pain. And to think this gift is within each of us and is free (no prescriptions needed)!

Laughter has some physical payoffs. It strengthens heart muscles and lowers blood pressure. It even improves face value!

When we can laugh at ourselves, we help ourselves and others to relax. Laughter relaxes our muscles, and the need to be perfect disappears very quickly. We find ourselves becoming childlike, and it just feels good to exercise our organs with the energy of our laughter.

Friedrich Nietzsche said, "To laugh means to love mischief." Mischief is so often limited to the world of children and barred from the adult world. Yet mischief makes us alive and likeable and creative. The wonderful thing about mischief is that it cannot be enjoyed alone, so we immediately get connected with others. Now, two worlds and two hearts and two souls are touched with new life.

36
Dragon Boat Races

Recently, I had the opportunity to go to China. It was truly a marvelous experience. While I was in Taipei, the Dragon Boat Festival occurred, an exciting and colorful event that is very meaningful to the people of China. It was evident from all the people who were lining the riverbank that this was a holiday people attended each year.

The custom of the Dragon Boat Festival centers around the story of Chu Yuan (340-278 B.C.), a counselor to the king of the state of Chu, in a turbulent period in Chinese history known as the Era of the Warring States. Chu was a very loyal courtier and a talented man of letters. He wanted to help his king do a better job of governing his country and was very much trusted and respected by the king.

Some courtiers became jealous and began to speak ill of Chu. The king listened to these maligners and began to distance himself from his loyal courtier. Chu was soon completely ignored by the king. Even though he wrote poems to express his loyal feelings to the king, he was exiled. Chu's departure from the capital was soon followed by the annexation of his country by the Chin state. When Chu heard of this, he was so saddened that he committed suicide by jumping into the Milo River.

When Chu's neighbors and friends heard about his suicide, they tried to rescue him by rowing boats to where he had disappeared under the water. Having failed, they then tried to save his body from being devoured by the fish by throwing balls of rice wrapped in seaweed into the water in hopes the fish would eat that mixture instead of their friend's body.

Perhaps the story of Chu Yuan is only a legend. Yet, the Chinese value it. The legend that people tried to save Chu Yuan by immediately going to the place where he drowned eventually evolved into the Dragon Boat Festival. The balls of rice thrown into the river to feed the fish created the custom of making tsung tzu, a clump of glutinous rice with meat and egg yolk wrapped in bamboo leaves.

We can learn much from this legend. Chu was passionate in what he valued and believed, and the mistrust and rejection by the king was the worst betrayal for him. The core of Chu Yuan was wounded and scarred to the point where he could see no other options for his life.

Although Chu attempted to express himself through his poetry, his words went unheard by the king. This was the ultimate devastation for the loyal servant.

37
Letting Go

Today is all we have that is real. We cannot change the past. We cannot take back a word we've said. We cannot redo a thing we've done. The only thing we can change is the way we feel about the past.

We do not have a lot of control over the future either. We can plan for tomorrow and hope our plans are actualized, but we cannot make everything happen our way.

Yet so many of us are controlled by our yesterdays and tomorrows. As a result, we lose our todays. There is no energy in our past or in our future. Our energy is grounded in the present.

Thinking back on painful experiences is like living the experience again. It is giving to the experience a lot more power than necessary. It is keeping the situation or experience alive.

We really are hurting ourselves when we choose to hold on to those memories. We are empowering the past but not empowering the present. As we stay stuck in those memories, we exhaust ourselves.

Does it change it to relive it over and over for years? Of course not. The only thing it does is keep us out of touch with now and the opportunities right in front of us so that we are not truly living.

Some of us hold on to childhood memories and beliefs, allowing them to define who we are. Maybe we didn't feel smart enough or loved enough as children. Does that mean we have to dislike ourselves forever? Are those our excuses so we can behave inappropriately? Does that justify our moodiness or our lack of communication with others?

Holding on to negative thoughts and experiences only gives us a negative view of life. Unfortunately, others get victimized by such actions and words of ours.

Forgiving our past and letting go of what drains us is opting for fully living each moment. At times, this forgiving needs to be ritualized by going to another person and asking for forgiveness. Old feelings that are deeply imbedded in us need to be resurfaced, owned, and then replaced with other feelings.

If we have hurt others, it may be necessary to go to them and ask for their forgiveness. If it is not possible to do that in person, then we may have to do it in our thoughts—have a conversation with them, resolve those feelings, and then let go of them.

The next step is forgiving ourselves. That's not always easy. It is not easy to forgive, let go, and move on. But the alternative is to let others continue to hurt us or to continue to let ourselves be hurt. To break the cycle of pain, we must be in control of ourselves and not let others be in control of us.

There is a wonderful story of how monkeys are caught in Asia. There is a specific kind of monkey that searches for a special kind of nut to eat. The people create a box with a hole in the front and place that nut inside. When the monkey smells the nut, it reaches inside to grab it. Once the monkey has the nut in its fist, it cannot get its hand out of the hole because its clenched hand is too wide for the opening.

All the monkey has to do is let go of the nut so it can pull its hand out of the box and be free. But the monkey holds on to the nut and is captured.

We hold on to things, too, instead of letting go of them and freeing ourselves. These un-freedoms are our hurts and disappointments. They keep us from believing in ourselves and hold us back in nurturing who we are. We do not see ourselves as we are.

- We are always changing.
- We need to value who we are and who we can become.
- We need to be gentle with ourselves and to respect ourselves.
- We need to let go of the past and to forgive.
- Forgiveness is a conscious act.

38
Not Fitting In

There are times we feel we just don't fit in. We try our best. But when we compare ourselves with others and the way they dress and wear their hair and the kinds of cars they drive, we feel inferior. We begin to question our value and self-worth. Everyone else seems so competent. It seems no one else makes mistakes or messes up things quite as much as we do. It's hard to surface positive things about ourselves. No one seems to state anything worthwhile or positive when we need to hear it. And even if they do, we just don't hear it.

Sometimes, we try to fit in places that really are not for us. We may stay in those places for years and become frustrated and depressed. No matter what we do, it doesn't change a thing. We just don't fit. We are different.

Maybe we need to begin to look at ourselves rather than other people or the situations in which we find ourselves. That takes a lot of honesty and sincerity. It is also very risky. If what we find isn't right, then it may mean we have to leave, do something else, or go to another place. How frightening!

There is a wonderful Chinese fable about a man from the state of Lu who was skilled in weaving hemp sandals and his wife who was adept at weaving fine silk. The couple decided to move to the state of Yue in the south.

"You will be in dire straits," the man was told.

"Why?" asked the man of Lu.

"Hemp sandals are for walking, but the people of Yue walk barefoot. Silk is used for making hats, but the people of Yue go bare-headed. If you go to a place where your skills are utterly useless, how can you hope to do well?"

Like the couple from Lu, we sometimes put ourselves in situations that set us up for failure.

The Chinese tell another fable about a man who lost his axe. This man suspected his neighbor's son of stealing it. To him, everything about this boy—the expression on his face, the way he walked, the manner of his speech— betrayed that he had stolen the axe.

Not too long afterward, the man found the axe while rummaging through his cellar. The next time he saw his neighbor's son, nothing about the boy's behavior or appearance seemed to suggest the boy had stolen the axe.

What changed?

Our opinions and judgments seem to fit for us, but they are sometimes a bit off base. Our blurred vision hampers and stifles us. It is with openness and the ability to see more than one option that we grow. But change is not easy. It can even be painful.

There is a story about an old man who lived beside a very busy intersection and named his servant boy Fighter and his dog Biter. For three or four years, no one ever came to visit him. The old man wondered why and began asking. Someone finally told him the truth. When he changed the name of the servant boy and the dog, he had a stream of visitors.

What if that man had never asked? What if he had chosen to live in his little enclosed world? He would have deprived himself of life and laughter.

What changed?

39

A Chorus Line

Broadway shows are wonderful experiences. They entertain us and even bring us to tears. Melodies of the songs heard in Broadway shows are sung over and over, finding places in our lives.

A Chorus Line, the longest-running Broadway show, is my very favorite. The play is not like the usual Broadway spectacular. Usually, we go to Broadway shows to see the gorgeous scenery and costumes as well as to be exposed to the plot of the play. *A Chorus Line* is different. There are no costumes. There is no scenery. The play opens on an empty stage with a lot of nervous people standing there waiting to audition for a spot on the chorus line. Each person is living in her or his own world and telling herself or himself how much she or he needs this job.

Within the first ten minutes of the play, the director dismisses half of the participants and then tells the remaining group how he is going to pick the final chorus line. Each is told to stand on the white line drawn across the stage. When their names are called, they are to step forward and tell him who they are. He wants to know everything about them, not just their age and where they come from but everything they have ever done in life, good things and bad things. And based on that, he will pick the chorus line. Then the director comes and sits in the audience. It is only then that we see the mirrors on the backstage wall. Now the audience feels part of this play too.

The director calls the first person. She gives her name, says that she is twenty-two and comes from San Francisco, and has six brothers. She continues to mime her story.

Another nervous participant walks out and asks the audience, "What do I say? If I tell him I stole all that stuff, I'll never get the job. But if I don't tell him and he finds out, I won't get the job. What do I say?" And he continues to tell us his story.

Then the director calls another dancer. He steps forward, yells his name, and begins giving his data. Again, in mime. Another anxious interviewee steps out of line. He asks, "What do I tell him? Do I tell him I'm a homosexual?" He goes on to talk about his life.

The story of *A Chorus Line* is not about the people called forth but about the people who stand on the line and wait, about all those who tell us who they really are and are sometimes frightened they will not be accepted or chosen. This play is about a bunch of real people, people like you and me, who stand in front of others and wonder if they will make room for them, wonder if they will accept them.

The play runs two hours and ten minutes without an intermission. Near the end of the play, the director walks out on stage and asks all of them why they want to be in a chorus line. In reality, he explains, the play they are auditioning for won't last forever. It may go a few weeks or a few months or even a few years, but then they will have to get other jobs.

The dancers begin questioning themselves and trying to understand why they first wanted this job. It is at this point of the play we hear the very beautiful song, "What I Did for Love." The message is powerful:

> Kiss today goodbye,
> the sweetness and the sorrow.
> Wish me luck.
> The same to you.
> And I won't regret
> what I did for love, what I did for love. . . .

I remember leaning over to the person I was with and saying, "This is the best show I've ever seen."

Then the director takes charge once more: "All right, now I'm going to pick the chorus line. Everyone come and stand on the white line. As I call your name, please step forth." Slowly, painfully, the director calls half the group forth. He then states, "Second line, you're the chorus line. Report to work on Monday morning."

The first line of the stage members is devastated. Now I leaned over to the person I was with and said, "This is worst show I've ever seen.

She quickly reminded me, "You just said it was the best."

"I know," I answered, "but it's also the worst."

The story of *A Chorus Line* is the story of all of us. It's the story of real people who stand in front of others all the time. We tell others who we are and become vulnerable. It is very risky telling others who we are and what we need. It lets others know things about us that we often hide deep inside.

As the actors walk off the stage, we find ourselves totally involved with all of them. We know who they are and the secrets they have kept locked inside for so long. These people are not strangers. We feel intimately involved with them. We find ourselves talking to them:

"Don't tell that about yourself. No one cares."

"You're a good person."

"I'm so glad you shared that with us."

These dancers want and need the job. They are passionate in their desire to be hired. They doubt themselves. They reveal themselves. They risk being transparent. And some of them know they will not be chosen. Some of them know this risk is in vain.

Once we tell others something about ourselves, it is not possible to take it back. Denial is not possible. Once we've been vulnerable, it is never the same again.

What happens to us when we take that risk? What is the result of our soul-searching shared? Or do we choose to remain closed and keep our secrets locked inside for only us to know?

It is possible for us never to open up to anyone, but the price is great:

- It means we never grow close to others.
- It means we lock up inside who we are and never become who we could truly be.
- It means we never give birth to parts of us that require risk and sharing and vulnerability.
- It means we do not choose life or living.

40
Make Some Mistakes

Somewhere along the line, we began to believe that we should be perfect, that we should never make mistakes, that we should always do everything right.

These kinds of messages are unhealthy because they take away creativity and wholeness. We lose spontaneity, we limit our abilities, we discount any newness, we never learn how to play or to relax or to enjoy ourselves. Our lives become so fixed on agendas and things we "have to do" that we never learn to develop free spirits. We censor our creativity and lose sight of joy and the moments of energy that are present in our day.

Until we learn to make mistakes and laugh at ourselves, we are prisoners, and our own jail-keepers. We have to stop being so hard on ourselves and begin to respect and like ourselves. I'm not just suggesting that we love ourselves but also that we *like* ourselves. Liking ourselves implies that we know ourselves and take care of ourselves and have learned to be gentle with ourselves.

It also implies that we are aware of the darker side of our personalities and are in touch with things about us that have sharp edges and, at times, irritate people. No one is perfect. There are always things about all of us that we could work on and improve.

Learning to make mistakes is possible, but we have to set out to learn the skill. It means being uncomfortable with ourselves for a while. It can feel awkward and stifling. But once we learn how to make mistakes, we stop being so hard on ourselves and on others too.

Here is a homework assignment for the rest of your life: Make three mistakes a day on purpose. Anything over and above that earns bonus points, and you can score as many bonus points as you would like during each day. But you must make three mistakes a day on purpose.

What you will begin to do is breathe easier. You'll take a lot of pressure off your own shoulders. After a while, you'll begin to see that you are easier on others and not so quick to judge their actions or intentions. The payoff is refreshing. You'll find you have more patience and are not as tense. You'll smile more (so the environment is now enriched).

Carry a little ruler in your head and picture it numbered from one to ten. Decide not to give every action of your life—or of the lives of those with whom you are interacting—a score of eight, nine, or ten. Sometimes, the behavior only deserves a one, two, or three. Reserve some of your energy for things that really need attention. Is a spilled glass of milk really deserving of an eight, nine, or ten explosion? Do you really want to spend so much energy on a slammed door or a misplaced set of keys?

There is a wonderful principle that states: "Things worth doing are worth doing poorly." If we could only learn that instead of thinking that we have to do everything. It is possible and healthy just to use whatever time we have available to us. But we were taught just the opposite and learned that the things worth doing are to be done perfectly and properly. Sometimes, we just don't have the time to do a total job, and we only raise our own frustration level if we wait until we have time to do the complete task.

We look out at our gardens and think we have to go out and pull out all the weeds. Why don't we just pull out the big ones?

When we are having company, we think we have to polish all the silverware. Why don't we just polish what we are going to use that evening?

When we think that way, tasks become accomplishable, and we take reaching perfection out of our expectations.

Mistakes teach us to relax. They teach us that perfection is not everything. We can learn a lot when we make a mistake. Sometimes, we even find out that there is another way of doing something that ends up superior to the one solution we thought possible.

41

A New Way of Looking

The Chinese character for "opportunity" is the same character they have for "crisis." It's up to us to perceive the happenings in our lives as opportunities or as crises. We may not be able to control a situation or event, but we do have control over the response we choose.

For example, perhaps we plan a big picnic, and it begins to pour. We cannot control the rain. We can decide, however, if we want to get depressed, helpless, and angry. A different option is to find a creative solution and hold the picnic in another spot or to change the time or day.

Or maybe we are driving on a major highway and miss our exit. Loads of choices are ours. We can lose control, scream and yell and pound the dashboard. We can swear and blame the passengers in the car, reminding them that if they were paying attention we would have seen the exit approaching. Or we can drive to the next exit, turn around, and return to the correct exit.

The response to a situation or event is ours. The choice we make determines the outcome of the moment. So, if we don't like the outcome, all we have to do is change our response. The situation or the event is what we tend to blame, but the power to make that choice is ours.

To be able to experience the joy and positive energy in the moment, it is important to remember that we control our thoughts. We have 50,000 thoughts a day. We have to decide which ones we want to hold on to and let control our actions.

It is important to keep our self-talk positive and not buy into the negativity that can harm our psychological thought process. When we make a mistake or miss a turn, we may want to remind ourselves that it is not the end of the world and that nothing terrible is going to happen.

We may not be able to control what happens or the outcome of the situation, but we can decide how we want to behave and act and think.

12

Healthy "I" and Healthy "We"

Relationships are funny things. We can't live with them and we can't live without them. They are capable of bringing both joy and sadness into our lives. They can bring us energy or they can drain us. We cry because of things that occur in our relationships, and we laugh together in the same relationships.

We do not have many positive models for relationships in our culture. What we often see are unhealthy relationships. We see abuse and violence and dysfunctional patterns. We witness people casting away relationships.

Divorce occurs on many levels: People stop talking to each other. People go years without even remembering what caused the division between them. Some find themselves lonely because they shy away from intimacy and closeness. Others are afraid of commitment and go from one relationship to another, inventing reasons not to bond.

Enduring the growth of a relationship has been lost in a culture that thinks things should happen quickly and easily or that maybe it's not worth it. Just looking around our kitchens we see electric can openers, dishwashers, microwave ovens. They all imply a "hurry-up" attitude.

We no longer sit on our front porches in rocking chairs and enjoy conversations with family members and friends. Instead, we blast our televisions and radios and walk around with headphones glued to our ears.

What are we afraid of? Is it life itself? Is it each other? Is it ourselves?

Relationships take a long time to mature. Adolescents often think if they go out twice with someone, they are "going steady." The art of building friendships and relationships is lost. Often, people jump into sexual relationships and don't take the time to build relationships on other levels. "Dear Abby" had a "Gem of the Day" quote in the newspaper that could challenge all of us: "It takes a long time to grow an old friend."

When we begin a relationship, we get into an enmeshment stage. During this time, we lose the concept of self and tend to identify ourselves in relation to the other. During this stage, we have intimacy but no autonomy. We experience a lot of closeness. However, we do not set any personal boundaries. This is a very romantic model. It appears to be like love. It is at this stage that we see dependent relationships. It is also during this stage that people can't choose to love the other since they need the other. Negative feelings are not expressed at this stage.

While in the enmeshment stage, thoughts of the other person are very frequent. People call the other a thousand times a day. They bring home flowers and gifts. Cards are picked out especially for the other.

The problem is that it is impossible for both people to remain in this stage. Inevitably, one will outgrow it. When that occurs, people have a tendency to jump to disengagement. Now there is no closeness. There is a lot of autonomy but no intimacy. This stage is defined as the "I do my thing; you do your thing" stage. It is here we find divorce, and divorce happens in all kinds of relationships—marriages, families, friendships, work.

We have to find the balance of mutuality. This stage requires both autonomy and intimacy. We can have our own identities and think our own thoughts and make our own decisions. We can't have a healthy "we" unless we have a healthy "I." But neither can we have a healthy "I" unless we have a healthy "we."

The following are a few suggestions to help create healthy relationships. Remember that relationships take a lot of work; none of these is meant to be used individually. It takes two people giving about eighty percent to each other to maintain any relationship. This list is for all kinds of relationships—marriages, significant others, friends, family members, God, community members.

Develop intellectual intimacy with each other. Intellectual intimacy is how we talk to each other. It is sharing thoughts, ideas, and opinions with someone we want to be close to. We can talk about politics, religion, and the headlines in the news. We can discuss conditions of society, schools, and families today. The topic is not important. It is the talking and sharing that begin to bond us. We begin to relate to each other. We sometimes forget to keep this process going when we begin getting used to each other.

In the early days of getting to know each other, we talk about almost anything just to be able to spend time with the other. As we get more comfortable with the other and get to know patterns of behavior, we talk less and less. Intellectual intimacy challenges us to stay in touch with the other. This is information that we learn from others or from the television or newspaper, so it is not very threatening. Everyone is entitled to his or her own opinion.

We can get closer to each other as we share feelings with each other. Feelings are a different level of communication and far more risky to share than intellectual thoughts. We have a tendency not to share our feelings because we are much more vulnerable with the person to whom we reveal our feelings. However, to be close and have a healthy relationship with another, it is essential that we share this part of ourselves with the other. There is no way we can truly know ourselves or another person unless we share our feelings.

Sharing the values of the other is another way we can be bonded in a relationship. It means knowing the other and appreciating his or her interests. These values do not need to become ours. They are the interests, loves, and lifelines of the other. But we must learn to appreciate them. If our significant other enjoys music, then it is important that we (once in a while) go to a concert or listen to an important piece of music. If we like movies, then it is a reasonable request that the other (once in a while) go to a movie with us. Doing so even gives us something to discuss on an intellectual sharing level.

Values are at the core of who we are, so it is essential to share our values with people we love and for those same people to share their values with us. It is important that there be some common values also. These are the things both can then experience and enjoy together. We can begin to identify our values by looking at how we spend our time and money. What are the ways you use your free time?

The "why" of anything tells about values. For instance, ask yourself what is your favorite television show and "why"; what is your favorite food and "why";

what is your favorite vacation place and "why." It is not your answer that helps you get to know yourself; it is the "why" behind it. To be able to be ourselves and not have to disown our values to please another is what intimate love is all about.

Look at your own trust levels in relationships. We cannot get close to others or laugh and share life unless we trust others. Sometimes, our capacity for trust is stilted by our own early upbringings. How we grew up, how we felt loved, and how we experienced security are all essential for us to know ourselves and then to be able to share with those with whom we choose to be close and intimate. Family secrets can block us in our ability to give ourselves to others. This is not to imply we should be open books for everyone, but it is meant to be a red flag in relationships if we never reveal who we are to another.

The capacity for trust is also influenced by our own experiences with love. If we have been hurt or scarred in love relationships, we may not be too willing to enter another one for fear that this may happen again. It is helpful to reflect on our own history of relationships and to be aware of positive and negative aspects of these past relationships.

Learn that differences are not bad and can truly enhance a relationship. Learn all you can about the interests of the other and leave room for different likes and activities.

Let the other person make mistakes. Don't be so fast in putting others down. We need to affirm each other and not disregard or judge each other.

Don't bring past resentments or arguments into the present. No one can change what happened yesterday. To keep nagging or bringing up what another did or didn't do changes nothing.

Forgive the other. Forgiveness is a conscious act. It is not a feeling. Decide that you care enough about the other that you can forgive and let go. Remember that forgiveness and the ability to forget are not the same. We don't always forget the behavior, but we can still forgive.

Hug and touch. From birth, we have physical needs. We all need to be touched and hugged. In a relationship, it is essential to put our arms around the other person once in a while. Physical expressions of love speak volumes of words. This physical intimacy is different from sexual intimacy. No one can survive without physical intimacy.

The words "I'm sorry" are not a sign of weakness. They are a sign of courage and strength. To admit when we are wrong takes courage. However, we can mistakenly believe that saying, "I'm sorry" is all that's needed. To say it once is fine, but after that, a behavior must accompany the words. For example, if a waiter spills hot tea on someone's arm and says, "I'm sorry," we hope he is, but it is not enough. That person's arm must be attended to.

Clarify expectations. What do we expect from others? What do others expect from us? Are these real or unreal expectations? Can we be open to change any expectations that are unreal? If not, we will remain frustrated.

Relationships need to have self-revelation from both people. That takes time. Time must be spent nourishing and nurturing the relationship. Time is needed to celebrate the relationship. It is in using this time together and focusing on the other that we can grow in a relationship.

Go slowly. Relationships mature slowly and must be nurtured gently.

43
Live Longer

Evidence suggests that optimists live longer than pessimists. It has been proven that optimists catch fewer infectious diseases than pessimists. Optimists have better health habits than pessimists. Even our immune system works better when we are optimistic.

We need to work on changing messages that create pessimistic attitudes. If we put ourselves down when we fail or think of ourselves as not good, we create negative thinking patterns that can destroy us. We learn how to be victims—and then we become helpless.

We have become a people who like to feel bad. People greet each other with itemized lists of how they feel: "I have such a headache. . . . My head is killing me. . . . I can't eat a thing. . . . My stomach hurts so much. . . . My back is breaking." It's no wonder that over-the-counter pain relievers sell so well in this country.

It has been documented that seventy-five percent of daily conversation is negative. Some people wake up in the morning and start the day complaining about getting up. Then the weather outside is never right. It's either too hot or too cold; it's raining or snowing. Immediately, these people begin thinking of things that they have to do. They begin dreading the trip to the grocery store. Of course, they will get into the line that moves the slowest and where the person in front of them uses a million coupons to save two dollars.

They fill their days with "have to's." There is no fun, no free time, no enjoyment. There are just things that must be done. No wonder such folks are exhausted a few minutes after they get up in the morning!

Here's a prescription we can fill ourselves:

- We have to teach ourselves to enjoy life again.
- We need to slow down long enough to be able to have a conversation with somebody else.
- We must smile more. Research has proven that how you look affects the way you feel. Even pretending to be happy gets you to feel happy.
- We need to spend time eating with people, and talking and listening to each other.

But we have become a culture of convenience, so we rush every place. We have cellular telephones so we never have to wait or find a phone. We use our microwave ovens so our dinners will be ready in three minutes so we can swallow them in two minutes. We have lost the art of enjoying food. Instead of sitting at our kitchen tables and sharing the stories of our day, we eat on the run. We have become more interested in the fat content of our food than in the nourishment that food provides the body, soul, and mind.

To live longer, we must live one minute at a time—truly live each. For some, that may mean living one second at a time. We must take to heart these beautiful words: "Yesterday's the past, tomorrow's the future, but today is a gift. That's why it's called the present."

11

Bifocals and Trick Knees

We live in a world of instant information. Every day something new is printed to tell us how we can stay healthier. There are diet clubs and nutrition newsletters and talk shows galore on this topic. We are told that the slower the background music, the less people tend to eat at a meal. All one has to do is watch an adolescent and listen to his or her background music to validate that statement.

We've held some myths for years that we need to unlearn in order to be healthier. For instance, we now know that spicy hot foods do not cause or aggravate ulcers, and crackers and potato chips may be more likely to cause cavities than stickier foods such as caramels and raisins. As we learn and relearn this information, we can make some new choices. Oddly enough, some of these choices are freeing. Others are delightful!

To experience joy in our lives, we must remember that we are connected to everything. We are in tune with the universe and the stars and the earth and the mountains and the oceans. We need to be one with ourselves and to have a healthy respect and reverence for who we are. We have to be able to celebrate our gifts and talents while acknowledging our faults. We need to be in good relationships with other people.

We are social beings who are not created to be alone. We need to be connected to other people. This is essential for us to be able to truly believe in who we are.

None of us can really know who we are unless we are validated by others. Someone can hope she is a good first grade teacher, but she can never really believe it unless someone validates that. This need for validation keeps us connected to each other.

Relationships with others allow us to stretch ourselves and to learn to risk and to trust. It gets mighty risky sharing some deep, intimate feelings with others because we become vulnerable when we open ourselves up to someone else. However, if this never happens, there will be a part of us that is never alive. We must nurture and be nurtured. Joy can never come into our souls if we remain isolated and separate from others.

To have this joy, we must also have a belief in a power beyond ourselves. Wholeness calls us to be connected to our God. Joy is not connected to material possessions, nor is it measured by our accomplishments.

Joy has nothing to do with what other people think of us. Joy is an inner state of being that gives life itself to our souls. It is woven into the very quality of our lives. It is like the breath that keeps us connected to ourselves and to others.

Some people find it threatening to realize that they need to be involved and connected to others. But Dr. Renee Spitz discovered that if human beings do not get significant recognition from others, their spines quite literally shrivel. They become increasingly withdrawn from relationships.

An awareness of this fact puts a responsibility on all of our shoulders. It is important that we affirm and acknowledge other people who are in our lives.

Life is not a free ride. We all have to do our part. We need not only to be recognized, but also to recognize those in our lives. We are not in this alone. What a wonderful thought! We need other people and others need us!

Maybe it's not so bad that as we age, many of us need bifocals. There is quite an adjustment with such things as the awkwardness of walking up and down stairs and reading newspapers, but perhaps bifocals are just the reminders we need that we always have the ability to re-shape our vision. Bifocals are a reminder that we always have the ability to look at things differently and see different perspectives.

Aging, and even bifocals, can be a real gift. Aging is often intertwined with disease, but they are not the same. The average age of people admitted to nursing homes is not sixty-five or seventy, but eighty. Only five percent of the population is in some kind of institution, whether acute hospital, convalescent hospital, mental hospital, or nursing home. A recent Harris poll reported that only a little more than twenty percent of older Americans said they were debilitated by health problems. Recent research by the National Institute on Aging suggests that many of the problems of old age are not due to aging at all but to improper care of the body over a lifetime. Eighty percent of the health problems of older people are now thought to be preventable or postponable.

There is a story of an eighty-two-year-old man who went to the doctor with the complaint that his left knee was painful and stiff. The man told the doctor that he just couldn't get comfortable. He couldn't stand or sit, and the knee was aching constantly. He asked the doctor to do something to relieve the pain. The doctor examined the man's knee and said, "Well, what do you expect?

After all, it's an eighty-two-year-old knee." The patient looked at the doctor and said, "Sure it is, but so is the other one, and it's not bothering me!"

The more we talk about wellness and wholeness, the more we begin to understand the importance of keeping ourselves mentally alive and healthy. Most losses in mental capacity happen to the very old, not to people in their sixties, seventies, and eighties, and those losses are due not necessarily to age itself but to depression, drug interactions, lack of exercise, or other reversible conditions.

Brain-scan studies conducted at the National Institute on Aging and based directly on metabolic activity have shown that the healthy aged brain is as active and efficient as the healthy young brain. Study after study has shown that people who stay active and intellectually challenged not only maintain their mental alertness but also live longer.

If only we would heed the words of anthropologist Ashley Montagu when he suggested that we should all try to "die young as late as possible." And we could all learn a lesson from comedian George Burns, who said: "You can't help getting older, but you can help getting old."

Joy and humor can be a wonderful way of adding years to your life, as well as life to your years.

45
Accent on Stress

Stress is a killer. It affects the quality of many lives. It would be impossible to find someone in the world who does not experience some level of stress and anxiety. But stress can be dealt with, and if we don't deal with it, it begins to deal with us.

There is a positive stress called "eustress." It helps us to function and to get things accomplished. It's the stress we all feel when we walk into a dinner party or a meeting and begin to wonder if we will know anyone or if we will feel out of place. It is the stress we feel when we've just started a new job. It's the stress experienced at the birth of a baby. It's the stress a student feels when writing a term paper. We've all had similar experiences and know the effects of this type of stress on us.

Stress is the body's physical, mental, and chemical reaction to circumstances that excite, confuse, frighten, endanger, or irritate us. Stress can be caused by an identified or unidentified stressor or by a stressful event. It is impossible to go through life without stress since stress prepares us to handle things that are unfamiliar or things that appear to threaten us.

Faced with a crisis—emotional or physical—the human body has a fairly standard physical reaction: arousal hormones pour into the blood stream . . . the heart beats faster . . . blood pressure rises . . . the lungs suck in more oxygen . . . more sugar circulates in the blood to provide energy. This is the "Fight or Flight" response that gets the body ready for action. But if the strain continues, it is very possible that a serious illness may result.

Not everyone reacts to stress the same way. Some people thrive on stress while others fall apart under it. Researchers have discovered that it's mostly a matter of how people handle it. There is ample evidence to prove that stress can contribute to various medical problems such as heart disease, high blood pressure, ulcers, asthma, headaches, and even the common cold.

"Eustress" is the stress of winning. It comes with a sense of achievement, triumph, and exhilaration. "Distress" is the negative stress. This is the stress of losing. It occurs when one senses a loss of feelings of security and adequacy. Disappointments, feelings of desperation, and a sense of helplessness can trigger distress.

People today are feeling a great deal of stress in relation to the workplace. They take on too much for too long and too intensely. Then they begin to feel a lot of pressure, which can come from three places: within, without, and administration.

People feel pressure from within to accomplish and to succeed. The pressure they experience from without is from the population they are trying to serve.

Administration pressures people by demanding and judging on statistics and playing the numbers game. When that happens, people begin to feel guilt. As a result, they put in more and more hours, put forth more effort, and try harder and harder.

Thus people begin to work harder and become more exhausted, frustrated, irritable, and cynical in their outlook and behavior. This results in less effective people.

Hans Selye, who has been called the "Father of Stress," attempted with the General Adaptation Syndrome to explain stress to us. There are three stages: the alarm stage, the stage of resistance, and the stage of exhaustion.

The alarm stage occurs when we first notice a stressor and prepare to fight it. This is the short period when the adrenaline starts to flow.

We then move into the stage of resistance. Our bodies give us extra strength to get through the crisis period.

The final stage is exhaustion when the crisis is over and we just can't go on anymore. If we don't plan time for the exhaustion stage, our bodies take over by getting sick and forcing us to take a rest.

Stress is going to happen to us, but it doesn't have to kill us. The following are a few suggestions for handling and dealing with stress.

Know what causes your stress. Identify the situations in your life that make you feel tense. This is a very important step but one we tend to skip over. We think we know the stress and never look at the cause of it. It's not the stress we know about that's going to get us; it's the stress we don't know about.

Identify your feelings. Feelings are important to understand because they determine our behaviors. Once we are aware of our feelings, we get an insight into our choice of behaviors.

Become aware of your body and such signs as headaches, tensed muscles, stomach upsets, cold or clammy hands, and clenched teeth. These are signals from the body that indicate the presence of stress in our lives.

We all respond to stressful situations either physically or mentally, or both physically and mentally. If your body wiggles and you can't sit still, then you respond to stress in a physical manner. If your mind goes thirty miles per hour and you can't concentrate, then you respond mentally to stressful situations.

Research has helped us look at the necessity of choosing behaviors that match our reactions. If you respond physically, then get up and walk slowly for about a minute or two. The anxiety will then begin to decrease. Then you can ask yourself what the stress is all about.

If your mind keeps going and you can't sleep, then open a book. This should be a book for entertainment and not something you are studying or want to remember. A good novel does the trick.

Read and read and read, and then you will begin to feel the anxiety subside. At that point, you can then ask yourself what is causing the stress.

If you respond both physically and mentally to stress, then put activities in your life that require both physical and mental reactions. Swimming, dancing, and playing tennis are examples of activities that require both physical and mental behaviors.

Memorize this: "Things worth doing are worth doing poorly." Obviously, this is not what we were taught. We believe that we have to have all the time necessary to complete a project or else we don't even start it. Hence, many things never get accomplished. We need to learn to use our time well. If we have only twenty minutes, then using that time guarantees that twenty minutes of the project gets done.

Ask yourself: "What's the worst possible thing that can happen?" It usually is not a catastrophe. The result may not be exactly what we want or expect, but it is not worth all the negative energy to worry about it.

Make a list of things that uplift you . . . things that bring a smile to your face . . . things that make you feel good and appreciated and cared about: a sunrise, a sunset, a compliment, getting an unexpected phone call from a friend, receiving a card in the mail or a letter from someone who is thinking about you, watching a humorous movie, having someone remember your birthday. Make up your own list. Then watch how some of those things happen, without your getting the mileage you could out of them. Use them. They really are stress reducers.

Listen to your own "self-talk." This is the talk or conversation that goes on in your head all the time. If self-talk is negative, then your stress level will remain very high. If you hear yourself being negative, change it to positive self-talk.

Check out your expectations. We have expectations for everything. We expect to drive home safely from work; we expect people we love to love us back; we expect people to be on time for appointments; we expect people to be honest with us—the list could go on forever.

The next time you get upset or frustrated, check out your expectations. When our expectations are not met, some type of crisis comes into our lives. This crisis usually takes the form of sadness, frustration, or anger.

Make a distinction for yourself between wants and needs. We do not "need" everything. We may "want" something, but we really don't "need" it. If you need something, you cannot live without it. We all need air, food, water, and physical touch. We do not need to drive fancy cars, own fur coats, or eat gourmet meals every evening. We may want those things, but we truly do not need them.

Develop a belief in your own competence. Everyone has some competence in some area. Some people can bake pies; others write books; some fly planes; others have computer skills; and many excel in sports. Find at least one thing you can do and celebrate that.

Change irrational thoughts and ideas into rational ones.
Some people cling to thoughts that bind them: "I have to
be perfect. . . . People should act the way I want them
to. . . . I have to have everyone's love and approval."
Messages like these lead to unhealthy and fragmented lives.
Change such irrational messages to: "It's human to make
mistakes and I'm not bad because I am not perfect. . . .
People act the way they want to act and not the way I want
them to act. . . . It would be nice to have others' approval
and love, but even without it I can still be okay." These
thoughts will offer a healthier and happier life.

Know your own support systems and creatively use them.
Find the people who are supportive of you and find ways
to connect with them. This connection does not have to
be time-consuming. A few minutes of conversation that
touches your heart is worth a fortune. Telephones, letters,
lunches, meetings, parties, and vacations are a few ways
of making these connections. Be as creative as possible in
making your own list.

Stay involved and active. Feeling productive reduces
stress. Don't just sit and listen to music; learn to play a
musical instrument. If you are not athletically inclined,
buy a season pass to a sporting event and cheer for your
team.

Organize your time well. Make a list of all the things
you need to accomplish each morning. Then number
them. Things that absolutely and positively have to get
done that day are number one. The twos on your list can
be important things but not essential. The threes are
things that will probably get on tomorrow's list. You
accomplish more items on your list if you take the time
to prioritize them. This also helps your self-esteem
because you feel good about all you accomplished versus
putting yourself down by reading your list at the end of

the day and making note of all the things that never got done.

Be clear. If the stress you are experiencing is a result of poor communication, then it is necessary to send clear, direct, honest messages to clear up the problem. Asserting oneself is a skill. It requires that you be in touch with your own choice of words and listen to your own tone of voice in sending a message.

But be clear about this: assertiveness is not aggressiveness. If you are aggressive, you really don't care about the other person. If you are submissive or passive, you really don't care about yourself; you think everyone else is more important. But when you choose to be assertive, you respect yourself and the other person. Then both can win.

Develop daily habits that contribute to health. Good nutrition and healthy eating are essential to wholeness and happiness. You should have some regular exercise in your daily routine. Good habits should include some play time. You need time to relax your muscles and clear the cobwebs out of your brain. Laughter does this well! You also need some relaxation in your daily routine. This may be time spent reading the paper or a book, or it may be sitting in a recliner doing nothing.

Get to like yourself. There are good things about you, and you should be proud of them. Affirm yourself. Pat yourself on the back.

Get enthusiastic. When we begin anything, we will always have a high level of enthusiasm. Think of a significant person in your life. Do you remember when you met that person? Wasn't he or she just wonderful? You might have found excuses to call that person several times a day, and sent cards and gifts for no reason. Try doing some of those things you used to do for that special person in your life and watch the relationship be energized.

Think of when you began the job you are in right now. Do you remember how you went home and told everyone how nice the place was and how special the people were who worked there? Enthusiasm can be regained.

Start identifying and appreciating differences in people. We sometimes get our stress levels high because we think differences are wrong or negative. Differences can enhance our relationships. A respect of differences can make our work places easier for all of us. Differences are not bad. The acknowledgment and acceptance of individual differences will decrease our stress and anxiety level. Remember that acceptance does not imply that you agree with everything. It is possible to accept someone and not agree with him or her.

46
Grieving and Loss

One of the most difficult things we have to deal with is facing the illness or death of someone we love. Our world changes instantly. It becomes focused on that person; all priorities are measured in relation to the loss we are experiencing or are about to experience.

Our bodies ache with pain. Our emotions are caught in our throats. Emptiness becomes a companion. Our actions become unconscious, and we go through our day routinely and robot-like. Things that used to mean a great deal are no longer important. People who could once tap our sense of humor no longer can reach us. Isolation feels safe. Depression offers security.

We begin to question everything and everyone: Why is this person sick? What is death? Why does anyone ever have to suffer? Is there really a God? Certainly God could never be kind and loving or it would never hurt this bad, we say.

Ignoring pain does not make it go away. We just transfer our feelings and possibly make things worse. Facing our feelings is not always an easy thing to do. But feelings are not right or wrong, and they will not hurt us. It helps if we can talk about our pain with someone we trust.

It tears us apart when we have to deal with the loss of a loved one. Sickness leaves everyone helpless. The unknown is always in front of us. Thoughts go through our heads at such a rate that we can hardly remember them and certainly cannot make any sense of them. We are angry at our own helplessness in not being able to aid the other. We are angry at the other for getting sick.

Then the circle widens, and we get angry at everyone. We even get mad at ourselves, asking: "Why is this happening? Why can't we do anything about it?"

We search for someone who can do something, but we can't find that person. We feel alone and isolated in our pain. Despair is close to us. We even begin to breathe differently. Our breathing becomes quite shallow. We decrease the amount of oxygen in our lungs and feel a lack of life in our bodies.

The thought of living without this significant person in our lives is just too overwhelming. We wonder, "How does anyone ever fill that empty space? Why would we ever want anyone to fill that space anyway?"

I was in the Philadelphia airport one time, enjoying a soda and a hot dog. (I always treat myself to a photography magazine when I'm traveling and devour it while munching a hot dog.) On this occasion, a man asked to share the table I was at. I moved my things closer to me to give him some space. He then looked at me and said, out of the blue, "I don't believe in God!"

I looked around to see who he was talking to and realized it was me.

I said, "You don't believe in God?" He responded, "No."

I wondered why he was sharing this with me. There were thousands of people in the airport. Why me? I didn't know the man. I was dressed in slacks and a shirt, and had no sign over my head that read: "Come talk to me. I'm lonely."

I needed to decide whether I was going to continue my ritual of eating my hot dog, drinking my soda, and reading my photography magazine or put that agenda aside and listen to this stranger for a few minutes.

I closed my book. He then told me his story:

He had a daughter who was very ill. The man was very wealthy and could afford any medical treatment for his daughter, but there was nothing anyone could do. To make matters worse, his daughter's husband was a doctor and his skills were not enough. This elderly gentleman said he had tested God by standing in front of a bush at his house waiting for it to burst into flames. It never did!

I listened as he relayed his despair and hopelessness. As we finished our "supper," he concluded, "I still don't believe there is a God. If there were a God, my daughter would be cured. If there were a God, the bush in front of my house would be in flames. If there were a God, there would be no calories in hot fudge sundaes."

As I walked away, I knew a bit more about him. He was no longer a stranger. He was anonymous, but he had shared his story and his pain.

He was vulnerable. And my heart was touched by his hurt and pain.

I walked to the gate from which I was departing and carried this man with me, my thoughts back at the table we had shared. I remembered the look in his eyes. I was grateful I had made the choice to listen for a few minutes to this stranger rather than continue the ritual of reading my photography magazine.

A few minutes later, he appeared by my side and offered me some candy. How did he find me? Where was he going? By some chance was he going on the same flight as I?

Again, I closed my book, realizing this conversation could go on only a few minutes since I would be boarding the plane soon. We also had assigned seats, so he would have to finish soon.

As the rows were called to board the plane, I said goodbye for the second time to this hurting man. Immediately on getting into my seat, I took out my photography magazine. Now it was time for me. I would read every word of it.

Only a few seconds passed before the person assigned to the seat next to me arrived. Guess who it was?

Right! The very same gentleman. Now I was beginning to question whether there is a God!

Again, I was confronted with the choice to read my magazine or listen. I closed my book, and he talked and talked and talked. I only listened.

As we landed in Albany an hour later, he turned and told me how good he felt: "No one has let me talk through this. Everyone wants me to feel better immediately. They all tell me how I should or shouldn't feel. You only listened. Thank you."

While walking down the aisle to exit the plane, he realized he had never told me his name. After he introduced himself, he asked my name.

"Sister Anne Bryan Smollin," I responded.

"You're a nun?" he said incredulously. "I told a nun I didn't believe in God!"

He turned to the gentleman across the aisle and said, "She's a nun, and I told her I didn't believe in God!" Others looked puzzled. Some smiled. Fearful we were going to get the entire plane into this personal discussion, I found myself inching my way off the plane.

"Do you need a ride some place?" my new friend asked.

"No, thank you," I answered. "My mother is going to pick me up."

After I greeted my mom, we walked toward the baggage claim area. The gentleman came over to my mom. "You have a wonderful daughter," he said.

Mom responded, "Thank you. I think she is wonderful too."

After walking a few more yards, Mom asked me, "Who is he?"

I answered, "I don't know. Someone who said he doesn't believe there is a God."

"But you told him there is a God, didn't you?" she asked.

"No," I said. "He already knows."

47
Amanda's Snow Cones

We all experience losses and must endure suffering through them. This process begins at birth and is, as a matter of fact, the first experience we have when we lose the security and protection of our mothers' wombs.

As our lives unfold, we continue to face losses. These losses have many faces: the death of significant people; friends moving away; the betrayal of false friends; physical losses such as sickness, loss of eyesight, loss of hearing, aging; and our personal losses.

The challenge for all of us is to cope and deal with loss, and to begin to allow the hurt to heal. This does not happen overnight. As a matter of fact, there is no single timeline for this process. Each one of us is different; we each walk and heal to our own drummer.

To begin dealing with a loss, we much first acknowledge it. It is important that we own the loss. Many try to deny it or hope the pain of it will go away. However, reality doesn't disappear, even when it's painful. We must talk about our losses and admit they are real.

Loss hurts! The pain can be intolerable. Denial doesn't make it disappear. Neither does ignoring it and saying, "Just don't think about it. There's nothing you can do about it." This attitude just prolongs the pain. Some people try to endure the pain alone and so internalize it.

These are the people who pay a price by getting physically sick and depressed.

For us to be healthy and happy, we must make a choice to deal with loss.

Acknowledging a loss implies being in touch not only with the loss itself but also with our feelings. It is all right to feel angry, to experience sadness, hurt, and resentment, to be disappointed and frustrated. We have a right to our feelings.

It is not unusual for people to experience numbness or a sense of shock when a loss occurs. These feelings deaden the pain. If we lose someone we love dearly, the numbness gets us through the initial stages. The feeling of grief usually follows this numbness. It is very important for us to release the pain through tears and not keep it bottled up inside of us in an attempt to be strong.

Next, it is common for people to experience a sense of being alone or forsaken. Often, that feels like depression. At this stage, we experience a helplessness or heaviness and do not feel like our normal selves. It is important not to anesthetize these feelings with unhealthy behaviors like eating too much or not at all, drinking to excess, smoking, sleeping too much or not at all. These only prolong our grieving process. These unhealthy Band-Aids do not deal with loss in a positive way. It is not uncommon at this stage to develop unhealthy relationships. People grab on to others hoping this will ease the pain of the loss. This is an attempt to fill a void that people experience because of the loss.

Physical symptoms can begin to surface. Headaches, loss of appetite, insomnia, and stomachaches are common physical expressions of unresolved grief. What scares people at this stage is that it is almost impossible to concentrate on anything. They begin to think they are "going crazy."

In an attempt to deal with the pain of loss, some people choose to hold on to guilt. Guilt is a way of not having to deal with anger. It's impossible to feel guilt and anger at the same time. Sometimes, the guilt is from what we said or did not say; this is an attempt to blame ourselves. Guilt can be irrational, exaggerated, and neurotic. We can certainly get stuck in guilt.

We can also choose to blame the other person for the loss. Then we will experience feelings of hostility and resentment. It ends up being the fault of someone else. We then feel we have the right to look sad, throw temper tantrums, sulk, and look unhappy. Sometimes, this is an attempt to make others feel some guilt or at least feel bad. It can be controlling and manipulative.

To deal with loss, we must learn to start again. Starting again offers us the ability to see options, to care, and to feel alive again. Dealing with a loss means letting go of our pain so the pain does not own us. Dealing with a loss means learning to forgive. All of this takes time.

Our losses include not only our separations and departures from those we lose but also our conscious and unconscious losses as well: our dreams, our impossible expectations, our illusions of freedom and power, and our younger selves.

We are constantly growing because we leave and let go and lose. We must mourn the loss of others and the loss of ourselves. The changes in our bodies redefine us. The events of our personal histories redefine us. We are always dealing with letting go: of our waistlines, our vigor, our sense of adventure, our 20/20 vision, our playfulness, our trust, our dreams.

The following are some practical ways of dealing with loss. Do not limit yourself to these suggestions.

Listen to yourself and others, and find what helps you through this process.

Identify the loss. Name it.

Look for options that are available to you.

Reinvest in your work.

Get re-involved in activities that are life-giving and happy for you.

Reconnect with friends.

Volunteer your time. Give some of yourself away. You'll feel connected to others. Volunteering also broadens your viewpoints and experiences. It helps give you a new perspective on things.

Realize that all people have limits. Look at your own limits realistically.

If you have a hobby or some special interest, spend some time developing it. If you need to, learn a new one.

Express your feelings out loud. Find someone you can trust and who can truly listen to you (and not just try to make you feel better or talk you out of your feelings). It's even helpful for you to talk about your feelings out loud to yourself. Talk to a mirror or just listen to what you are saying to yourself. This can help clarify what you are really experiencing.

Be kind to yourself. Do things you like to do. Treat yourself to your favorite meal.

Get plenty of rest. Physically and psychologically, people get drained when dealing with loss. Give yourself some extra rest time.

Take a course or learn some skill you have always wanted to take the time to learn.

Take all the hugs you can get. Hugs are worth a million words.

Set a few new goals. Beginnings have energy, and new experiences give us life.

Look at photographs and listen to music that has been important to you. It helps you look at the problem head on.

Remember that grieving and dealing with loss takes time. It is a process. Be patient with yourself. Eventually, the process does end. It does not go on forever unless you let that happen. Sometimes, you get more by holding on to pain, so you never let go. Maybe this gets you more attention or offers you an excuse to stay removed and nonproductive. But loss and grieving do end. Then something new comes to us.

Perhaps that's the message of the silkworm. The silkworm comes from a seed about the size of a grain of pepper. When the warm weather comes and the leaves begin to appear on the mulberry tree, the seeds start to live. The worms nourish themselves on mulberry leaves until, having grown to full size, they settle on some twigs. Then, using their mouths, they go about spinning the silk and making some very thick little cocoons in which they enclose themselves.

The fat, ugly silkworm then dies, and a beautiful little white butterfly comes forth from the cocoon.

Trying to understand loss and its pieces allows the pain to change. I learned this a while back when my father was hit by a car. The girl who hit him was on her way to bowling and never saw him crossing the street. My father never left the ICU of the hospital and died three months later. Throughout those months, we never heard from or met the girl who was driving the car.

Nine years later, I was giving a lecture and was seated at a large round table for dinner. All the participants had on name tags, and I began reading the names of the people at the table with me. Directly across from me was a woman who had the same name as the person who hit my father. Was she the same person? I dismissed the thought. After I finished the dinner talk, several people stood in line to talk with me. Toward the end of the line was the woman.

She said, "Was your father hit by a car on January 10, 1983?" As I said "yes," she burst into tears and said, "I am the one who hit your father." I quickly put my arm around her and told her how grateful I was that she came up to me and then started to fill in the pieces about his death. She already knew.

She said, "I was on my way bowling and wasn't paying any attention. All of a sudden, your father was in my windshield. I jumped out and started to yell for help, but there was no one around. I asked him not to die and took off my jacket and put it over him and kept asking him to wait for help."

I then decided we needed to get out of the room we were in, and so I started to walk out with her. I asked her to forgive herself. I tried to assure her that no one was holding it against her and that my father had died very peacefully. As we walked through the doorway, someone pulled me back for a second and the woman continued to leave the building. I don't remember her name anymore. It's not important anymore. But I will always be grateful that she told me she put her jacket on him and kept talking to him.

When you are dealing with loss, be sure to ask for help. This is not an easy thing for most adults. It is much easier to help someone else. But asking for help keeps you in touch with where you are. It also allows others to be there for you.

I learned this lesson from eight-year-old Amanda, who was very frightened while in the hospital. About a week after she went blind, the doctors decided to put in a central line to facilitate administering medication and food to her. Her mom left us alone in the hospital room so we could visit a while. As soon as Amanda found out we were alone, she began talking about some things that were bothering her. She finally got to talking about her fears about the central line. I admitted that I, too, would be afraid if I were having the procedure done and encouraged her to continue talking about it. She then taught me a wonderful lesson. She said, "Anne, teach me something so I don't have to be afraid."

I said, "Okay. Tell me someone with whom, when that person is with you, you feel safe and secure. You feel protected."

Quickly, she responded, "My mom."

I continued, "Now give me something—a thing—that when you have it, you feel good and happy. It brings a smile to your face and you feel the giggles inside too."

Just as quickly as before, she responded, "Snow cones."

I said, "Now do this with me. Tomorrow, they are going to come in and get you and put you on a stretcher and start to push you down the corridor. You'll feel scared and frightened—and that's okay. Now they're pushing you—and oh, look, Amanda, look who's coming down the hall toward you! It's your mom. And look, Amanda, what's that she has in her hand? It's a snow cone!"

Amanda smiled a smile that lit up the whole room and won my heart. She yelled, "Yeah, Anne, it's a rainbow snow cone."

Assuring her, I said, "Yes, it's a rainbow snow cone."

Amanda then said, "Stop, Anne. It works. It's okay."

A few minutes later, when her mother returned, Amanda said, "Mom, I want to tell you something so you don't have to be scared."

For Amanda, it worked. And all she had to do was ask!

48
A Special Meeting

I had the privilege of meeting a Sister of St. Joseph from Lithuania who was very elderly when I first encountered her. Sister Albertina served her God daily. She worked hard and was obedient to her superiors.

When I was in the Juniorate (a time when we already had taken first vows and were finishing our undergraduate degrees so we could then go out on a teaching assignment), Sister Albertina was our cook. From early morning until late at night, she could be found in the kitchen. Aside from the task of cooking for 135 people for every meal, she would say Rosary after Rosary after Rosary.

Each of us would take our turn to help prepare meals with her. When we reported to the kitchen, Sister Albertina would delegate the tasks so the meal would be completed for the scheduled hour. As we began mixing, stirring, and using up the leftovers, Sister Albertina would recite the Rosary aloud. Every so often, she would forget the mystery she was saying and ask, "What decade are we on?"

"Fifth" would always be the response. There are only five, and we hoped she would stop. But she just began the next five decades. Never was there a break from this routine.

Throughout the years, I grew closer to this holy woman, and my mother became her friend, companion, and family. Each week, they would visit nursing homes to bring some joy and caring to the residents. Sister Albertina would bring her relics and bless every person she met, whether they wanted it or not. It didn't matter. Neither did she ever consider whether anyone was Roman Catholic. Everyone got blessed.

When Sister Albertina could no longer go on this weekly venture, my faithful mother continued to visit her friend. The two of them would say the Rosary and the Stations of the Cross together as their relationship grew. When Sister Albertina became bedridden, my mother became her secretary and voice as she made Sister's daily telephone calls to shut-ins.

When Sister Albertina was dying, I was asked to come to our Provincial House as quickly as possible, since we were her family. One of the sisters with whom I lived accompanied me. As we walked into Sister Albertina's room, it was evident she had only a little more time on earth.

I pulled a chair next to the bed and took her hand. I told her how special she always had been to me (this was nothing new, for I told her this often) and how I always had depended on her prayers. That would never change.

One of her dear friends was then wheeled into the room: Sister Anna, who was blind and the same age as Sister Albertina. I moved over as they held hands. Sister Anna told her friend of the wonderful years they had shared. She recalled some of the difficult moments through which they had supported each other. Although we were listening to a monologue, it was a conversation between two women who had shared life, many happy moments, and many incidents of suffering.

Sister Anna then said to all of us present, "Let us say a decade of the Rosary. Which one should we say?"

I froze. The only mystery I could remember was the fifth. What if she asked me? I sat very quietly waiting for someone to rescue the moment.

"Let's say the Second Joyful Mystery," someone finally offered.

"Ah! The Visitation. When two women met and embraced and nothing was the same again." The wisdom of our elderly Sister Anna!

Some of us have been blessed by meeting someone and nothing ever being the same again. Such friends live forever in our hearts and souls.

They are the kind of people who, as soon as they are in view, bring a smile to our faces and warmth to our hearts. They are the kind of people who can live in another part of the world but are always near us. Once our lives are touched by someone special like that, nothing stays the same.

It's important that we cherish these relationships and nurture them. They are worth more than money or precious jewels. Their very presence is a present. Gifts like that are too valuable not to be protected.

49
Life's Gift

When we are born, the section of our brains that determines our sense of humor is only fifty percent developed. That means we have to develop the rest of it. How hopeful to realize we can become happier people who can learn to laugh more often and develop a sense of humor.

It has been proven that words have a major influence on our actions. One study found that when people were told that they had a good sense of humor, whether or not they actually did, they were so encouraged that they made many more attempts at saying or doing funny things than before they were praised. To me, this justifies being dishonest with certain people. You know, when people are miserable and have no sense of humor and no ability to see anything positive in the world—tell them what a wonderful sense of humor they have and how much you appreciate their seeing things in such a positive light! It's worth a try, especially if we can help negative people begin to discover the positive.

A wonderful Jesuit priest friend of mine, Fr. John Powell, has a note attached to the mirror in his bathroom. It reads: "You are looking at the face of the person who is responsible for your happiness today." Maybe we should all put that sign on every mirror in all our homes. We need to own that responsibility, to put into our lives things that are healthy and good and positive. It doesn't mean we see life through rose-colored glasses. It means we make choices not to dwell on and own and see only the negative.

There are some people whom we will never please. For some people nothing is ever right. If only we could remember that it doesn't pay for us to try to please everyone, perhaps we wouldn't waste so much time trying.

There's a wonderful story about a husband who always chose to be miserable. If his wife gave him orange juice, he wanted prune juice; if she gave him pancakes, he wanted eggs. Tired of always hearing him complain, she decided to fix two eggs for him one morning: one fried and the other scrambled. As the husband sat down at the kitchen table, he looked down at his plate. Seeing the two eggs, he looked up at her and announced, "You fried the wrong one." Some people are like that! But there is a saying, "When life gives you scraps, make quilts." The power is within us. Our response is always determined by our attitudes.

We can find subtle ways to let people know that we are not going to buy into pleasing everyone. Sometimes it is as easy as clarifying expectations. I have a sign on my office door that does just that. It states:

I can only please one person a day.

Today is not your day.

Tomorrow doesn't look any better.

You can borrow this for your door!

50

Check Your Attitudes

There is an old story about a man who came upon three masons working very hard at lifting up the heavy stones for the building they were constructing.

The man asked the first mason, "What are you doing?"

The mason looked up with anger and disgust, and replied, "What the hell does it look like? I'm working."

The man turned to the next mason and asked, "What are you doing?"

The second mason looked up, brushed the sweat from his brow, and replied, "I'm earning a living."

The man turned to the third mason and asked, "What are you doing?"

That mason looked up at the man with a glow in his eyes and replied, "I'm building a cathedral."

Which response fits you?

Are you the angry person who resents what is happening all around you and makes sure everyone knows it? Do you mutter comments under your breath or, even worse, loudly enough for another to hear? Do you call everyone and anyone "jerk" or "idiot" or some other word or phrase that lets them know they are wrong and you, of course, are right?

Sometimes, that tells us more about the speaker than the one on whom the speaker passes judgment. Listen to yourself and see if you are a judgmental person who puts down others. Listen to your responses as people ask you what you do or what you are doing. If you are not happy or do not like yourself, you'll hear it in your response.

Or are you like the second mason, earning a living and doing his job? Is your life middle-of-the-road, and are you doing only what you need to do—nothing more and nothing less?

Or are you like the third mason? The third mason projected the balance, pride, and focus that guarantee health and happiness. So often, the message is in the eyes! They glow and sparkle and generate energy. It is when the attitude is positive that we can be in touch with the reality of what is important to us.

51
The Worry Chair

Our parents have helped us know who we are. They gave us positive messages, and they gave us negative messages. Perhaps you grew up in a home environment where you were always told that you were dumb and stupid and never did anything right. If that was the case, then maybe today you still believe all those things. But you don't have to.

My mother always told me not only that I could do anything but also that I would do it well. I still believe that. One needs only to look at my calendar to see that I still believe I can do anything—and everything! But just hearing positive messages doesn't assure us that we always make healthy choices. The marvelous poet e. e. cummings reminds us, "It takes courage to grow up and turn out to be who you really are."

I once was handed a piece of paper that had only a quotation from Charles Swindoll, the author and lecturer, on it. It was titled *Attitude* and is one of those wonderful messages we can read over and over again:

> The longer I live, the more I realize the impact of attitude on life. Attitude, to me, is more important than facts. It is more important than the past, than education, than money, than circumstances, than failures, than successes, than what other people think or say or do. It is more important than appearance, giftedness or skill. It will make or break a company . . . a church . . . a home. The remarkable thing is we have a choice every day regarding the attitude we will embrace for that day. We cannot change our past. . . . We cannot change the fact that people will act in a certain way. We cannot change the inevitable.

144

The only thing we can do is play on the one string we have, and that is our attitude. . . . I am convinced that life is 10 percent what happens to me and 90 percent how I react to it. And let it begin with me.

Some people are born worriers. They worry about what happens if something doesn't work out right. They worry about what happens if it does work out right. They can even find some "what ifs" and "if onlys" and "maybes" to worry about in between.

Worry can be controlled. It is false to believe we can remove all worry from our lives. The secret is deciding when to worry. This can be done by determining a specific time or a specific place to focus on what we need to worry over.

Pick a chair in your house. Decide that the only time you will worry is when you are sitting in that chair. Then, when you find yourself getting anxious and your mind is beginning to race a hundred miles per hour tell your body that you are not going to think about what is worrying you until you are sitting in that chair. When you awaken in the middle of the night and you can't fall back asleep, tell your body you are not going to think about whatever is bothering you until you are sitting in that chair. Then roll over and fall back to sleep.

However, you must give yourself time to sit in that chair and worry every day. At first, begin with no more than a half hour. Do that for one week. Watch the way your body begins to believe you and gives you the choice of deciding when you will think and worry about what you want. Eventually, you can cut the time down until you will need only about five minutes each day. However, it is essential that you give your body and your mind that five minutes each day. What a small price to pay for twenty-three hours and fifty-five minutes of worry-free time every day!

There is another secret to dealing with worry: Stay in touch with *now*. So much humor, joy, and happiness go

145

unnoticed because we lose touch with reality. We walk around and lose focus. We can't see the trees for the forest. Perhaps one of the secrets is learning to be present to the *now*. We live so much in the future and the past that we miss the present moment—and that is where all the energy is.

Another trick for handling worry is to realize that our thoughts influence our emotions. If we are thinking of something that makes us smile, we feel good and happy. If we are thinking of something that frightens us, we become scared or upset.

Try it yourself:

1. Think of something or someone you love. What do you feel?
2. Next, think of something or someone you dislike. Now what do you feel?
3. Finally, think again of something or someone you love or who makes you smile.

You see, when we change our thoughts, our emotions quickly follow.

Milton wrote in *Paradise Lost*: "The mind is its own place, and in itself can make heaven of Hell, a hell of Heaven." If only we could believe in the power each one of us has for ourselves.

As we begin to control our own lives, we learn how to relax and how to enjoy our present moment. Then we learn quickly that the key to playfulness is a sense of humor. It's like magic. We create our good times and our sense of humor out of a frame of mind. This occurs when we find ourselves in situations that we enjoy and when we are in the company of people we enjoy. And those are choices we can make.

Mark Twain gave us another option for making our choices. He suggested that you "never put off till tomorrow what you can do the day after tomorrow."

52
Wobbling on the Tarmac

When our attitudes are negative, we begin to perceive ourselves very negatively, and we let our self-esteem be determined by those dark thoughts.

A client of mine was always putting herself down. Nothing she ever did was right. She lived in Albany, New York, and was once going to visit a friend in Fort Lauderdale, Florida. She had to fly from Albany and change planes in Philadelphia in order to get to Fort Lauderdale.

Step one went fine, but in Philadelphia she somehow got back on the same plane she had just left. That jet took her to West Palm Beach, instead of Fort Lauderdale. Those two airports are about twenty minutes from each other. At her next session with me, all she could say was how dumb she was and how stupid she was and how no one else had ever made mistakes like hers.

I tried to get her to see that this was not a crisis, that she hadn't suffered anything drastic. She had simply ended up at another airport which was only twenty minutes from where she was supposed to be. She could not hear that. To her, no one ever could have made a mistake like hers!

During the session, I tried everything I had ever learned in school (and even things I did not learn in school) to get her off this self-hatred. No luck! This went on for three sessions. It even got worse. I learned that once she had arrived at her friend's house in Fort Lauderdale, she never left it because she was afraid she would not be able to find her way back. How our fears can control us!

At the third session, I tried to put some reality into this scene for her one more time. I said to her, "I fell off a plane once!" There was no reaction, so I continued with my story.

I was on my way to Muskegon, Michigan, and I was supposed to go from Albany to Pittsburgh and then on to Chicago. There, I would change planes and go to Muskegon. When I arrived in Pittsburgh, however, they announced that the plane was not going on to Chicago. We had to get off and make other arrangements.

By the time I arrived in Chicago, I had missed my connection to Muskegon. They then took us by bus to a tiny airport—the kind that has no people, only a few vending machines. There, I decided to call ahead and tell the person picking me up what time I would be arriving. I opened up my folder to get the number of the CEO of the hospital at which I was giving the workshop only to find I did not have her home number, only the hospital number. I decided this was no problem because, surely, the hospital operator would be gracious enough to call her at home and relay the message.

I then opened up my wallet and found I had several bills but no coins. I decided I could call collect. The operator announced she had a collect call, but the woman answering the phone at the hospital quickly responded that she did not have the authority to accept it. I said,

"It's no problem. I will pay you tomorrow." She said, "But I can't. I'll lose my job!" I hurriedly said, "No, you won't. The CEO is a friend of mine." She again reminded me that she didn't have the authority to accept this collect call. I pleaded, "But I'm stuck in an airport."

By this time, the operator decided to get involved. She said, "She's stuck in an airport. Can't you accept these charges? She said she'd pay you back tomorrow." The woman helplessly responded, "I hope I won't lose my job." The operator quickly stated, "You won't. The CEO is a friend of hers!" Only because the operator helped me did the woman at the hospital finally agree.

After relaying the time-of-arrival change, I sat down to read a novel. When it was finally time to depart, we were led to a small plane in the middle of the airfield. Small? It was the kind of plane you crawl into, the type that holds five-and-a-half people! There is no distinction between the passengers and the pilot in these small planes. Everyone is in first class!

As we were departing the plane in Muskegon, the lone person who tripled as pilot, steward, and baggage-man chatted with each of us. Pointing at the floor by the exit door, he said to me, "Don't catch your heel on that piece of aluminum." Anyone can guess what happened. It's called the "self-fulfilling prophecy." I caught my heel on the piece of aluminum and fell down the whole flight of stairs.

As I tumbled, the thought that flashed through my mind wasn't, "How many bones am I going to break?" It was, "Don't ruin your outfit. It's the only one you have!"

I lay upside down on the stairs of the plane like a valise no one had claimed. When I got to my feet and leaned against the handrail, I turned to the gentleman behind me and told him I must have really clunked my head because I was so dizzy. I was rocking back and forth, unable to keep my balance, wondering if I had suffered a concussion.

The man told me, politely, that I hadn't suffered anything more damaging than losing the heels to both my shoes. Then he scrambled under the plane to retrieve them. I was tottering back and forth because of my shoes.

If anyone thinks that women's shoes become flat when the heels are removed, think again. Heel-less shoes become like boats. They pitch and roll—and I pitched and rolled with them.

I tiptoed from the middle of the field into the airport with the two busted heels clutched in the palm of my hand. Inside, I was warmly greeted by the CEO. She told me we were going to dinner at a restaurant of a friend of hers and that it didn't matter what time it was. I held my hand out to show her my two heels. She asked, "What are they?" I replied, "My heels. I fell off the plane!" Then we laughed loudly.

Now, I don't think I am stupid because I fell off the plane. I've done smarter things than that in my life, but I'm not dumb because I fell off a plane. You see, it's all in our attitudes and in what we tell ourselves about ourselves.

Our attitudes are learned things. If we become aware that we are holding on to negative attitudes, isn't it wonderful to know we have the power to change them? We never have to hold on to anything that drags us down. We can repair our attitudes as quickly as a cobbler can fix a pair of heel-less shoes.

53
You Are What
You Carry

We all have a tendency to hold on to things that destroy us and cause us to stay unhealthy. As a result, the heaviness of our burdens prevents us from enjoying life. We get caught up in negativity and depression. The world becomes dark and big. We see the world through blinders. Everything is perceived as black and white.

Letting go of our hurts and disappointments and learning to forgive ourselves and others are conscious acts. Forgiving someone or ourselves is not a feeling. It is a choice. We must choose to forgive.

Some people hold on to hurts and spend their whole lives being unhappy and miserable. Unfortunately, everyone who touches shoulders with such people senses the negative reactions and unhappiness. Who wants to be around someone who is always unhappy, always negative, always complaining? Still, these people hold on to this negativity and get some mileage out of it.

All of us get something—some payoff—when we hold on to things that are unhealthy. The unfortunate part is that, meanwhile, life keeps passing us by, and we miss all the healthy moments—moments filled with fun and laughter and positive energy. We get "stuck" in pain. This pain suffocates and strangles us, and we find ourselves not opting for life.

Some people hold on to words that were said to them years before. Some have not spoken for years to a person they loved for a reason they cannot even recall. People stay angry at others for days or weeks or years. Who pays the price for that? Only the person who holds on to the anger.

There is a marvelous story about two monks who were walking down a road and noticed a young woman waiting to cross a stream. One of the monks, to the dismay of the other, went to the woman, picked her up, and carried her across the water. He set her down, and she went on her way. The two monks then continued their own journey. About a mile down the road, the monk who was aghast at his friend's action remarked, "We are celibate. We are not even supposed to look at a woman, let alone pick one up and carry her across a stream. How could you possibly do that?" The other monk replied, "I put that woman down a mile back. Are you still carrying her around with you?"

We waste so much energy on old baggage, old thoughts, old hurts, old disappointments—and sometimes even other people's old baggage, old thoughts, old hurts, old disappointments. Our physical bodies don't hold on to dead skin. Every month—every twenty-eight days—we become new people. If only we could do the same psychologically. If only we could shed our old baggage, how healthy we would be.

I sometimes believe we work harder at living than we have to. We take 20,000 breaths a day. What are we choosing to breathe in? Negative things? Or are we consciously putting our energy into taking in positive air? Life-giving, pure, healthy air? We have learned to put those who smoke in a room by themselves so none of us has to allow that secondary smoke into our lungs. Can't we do the same with thoughts that are killing us—thoughts that are killing our spirits?

Recently, someone sent me a note card with a scene titled "The Brush Dance." The card revealed that "the Brush Dance was a Yurok Indian healing ritual where being true to yourself meant giving your best to help a person in need. Being true to yourself was the one and only Yurok Indian law."

Perhaps the simplicity of that culture can teach us something. Being true to ourselves implies that our priorities are in place. And while "self" is important, selflessness is a healthy part of self. No one of us truly knows how powerful and important we are or the true potential each one of us possesses. Think what could happen if we believed in ourselves and were aware of the strength and power we have.

In *The Compassionate Universe*, Eknath Easwarn shares with us a wonderful story about an afterschool conversation he had with his grandmother. They live in a small South Indian village, and although his grandmother has never been to school or learned to read, Easwarn writes of how he could not imagine anyone wiser. She is respected and loved by the entire village.

As his grandmother meets him at the gate after school one day, he tells her about what he has learned in geography class:

> "Granny," I began with considerable agitation, "scientists have discovered that our village is nothing but an anthill compared with the sun." As always, she listened carefully to everything I had to say. I told her about the vastness of outer space, the tremendous distances between planets, and the terrible smallness of the world that had up to then been my universe: our village, the nearby forest, the Blue Mountain on the horizon. "My teacher says we are just insignificant specks in the universe, Granny. We don't matter at all." Generally, my grandmother spoke very little, but her presence communicated a

tremendous security. She said nothing now. Calmly, she opened the gate, put her hand on my shoulder, and walked inside with me.

We sat down, and it was a while before she spoke. "No one is insignificant, son," she said finally. "Have you ever looked at Hasti's eyes?" Hasti was one of the elephants that frequently served in our religious ceremonies and that I had been learning to ride. Hasti's eyes, like the eyes of all elephants, were tiny, ridiculously small, really, for an animal so huge. "She has no idea how big she is," Granny said, "because she looks out at the world through such tiny eyes."

We all have the potential to be a Hasti. We, too, look out at the world through such tiny eyes. But in no way are we insignificant! I wonder what would happen if we believed that. I wonder what our eyes would see then. We do not know who we truly are, how wonderful we are, and the full potential we all have because, like Hasti, we are looking out through our own tiny eyes.

We could all use some wide-eyed excitement.

54
Tickle Your Soul

This chapter is meant to serve as an idea list on how to increase joy, laughter, and humor in your life.

Some of these are suggestions. Some are little strategies. Some will bring a smile to your face. Others will present a challenge to you.

Enjoy them—and then add your own ideas to the list.

Most important, promise yourself that you will do at least three conscious things a day to increase the joy, laughter, and humor in your life.

Here's my list:

Don't take yourself so seriously. Make at least three mistakes a day on purpose. Anything over and above that earns bonus points. Chalk up as many as you can. To be human means to make mistakes. Celebrate that gift of being human.

Ask for what you need. To be able to relax enough to see the joy in front of you, you have to realize you can't do it alone. To let others help you is a gift to them and a gift to you.

Smile more. It increases the value of your face. It also makes people want to be around you more. It may even make people wonder what you are up to.

Enjoy the now. Joy is in the present moment. Yesterday has no value. Tomorrow isn't here yet. The energy is only in this moment.

Give something away every day. I'm not talking about a material possession. I'm talking about a smile. A kind word. A spontaneous phone call to someone. A card or note sent to say you are thinking of someone.

Decide to live today fully. Don't die without having lived.

Spend some quiet time. It lowers anxiety and keeps you focused. There is enough anxious activity in our culture. The very human and holy art of being able to sit still is a spiritual behavior. Psalm 46 reminds us, "Be still, and know that I am God."

Learn to laugh at yourself. If you can't laugh at yourself, you are never free to see the humor in the paradoxes that occur in our daily lives.

Give yourself fifteen minutes out of each day that is your self-indulgence time. Use that time to do something that energizes your body with laughter. You can spend more time if possible, but you must spend at least fifteen minutes a day.

Make a list of twenty things that make you happy. Then make a contract with yourself to do at least three of those each day.

Learn to evaluate situations. What's the worst possible thing that can happen? Is it really as bad as you thought? It may mean a bit of an inconvenience or that you will not have something done exactly as you had planned, but does it have to become the end of the world?

Differentiate between wants and needs. There is a huge difference between them. If you need something, then you cannot live without it. Like oxygen, for instance. You need it to breathe. But do you really need that car? Or VCR? Or a person in your life to make you happy?

Make a list of things that uplift you. Be creative. Don't limit yourself at all. On my list would be things like a phone call from a friend, a sunset, a sunrise, and receiving a compliment. Once you become aware of things that give you a sense of being uplifted, you can get mileage out of them when they happen in your life. The reality is they happen every day—we are just not aware of them.

Believe in Santa Claus. Let the little child in you be real and alive. Giggle like a little child too.

Plan ahead. To have fun and do things you enjoy requires that you have these things in your life. That means planning on a daily basis. You are a worthwhile person, so be sure to put into your daily routine the events, people, and things that tickle your soul.

Give yourself permission to be "you." Sometimes, we need to accept ourselves where we are right then and there. Allow yourself some breathing space. Allow yourself some time to walk slowly or to limp through your wounds until you can learn to walk and run again.

Keep a journal and read through it every so often. You'll surprise yourself at your progress through your own journey.

Find a support group or a club that you can associate with that shares a common interest or concern. We are social beings. We need others. What a gift we give ourselves when we let others be there for us.

Find quotations or sayings or posters that are helpful to you. Display them where you can see them often. Your dresser mirror or bathroom mirror are good spots.

Don't waste your time on people who do not want to be in your life.

Keep a sense of balance in your life. Work, play, read, relax, rest, and pray.

Take your life one moment, one second, one hour, one day at a time.

Risk learning new things and developing new interests. Take time for activities that can bring some purpose to your life.

Don't waste your life with worry. Deal with what is real. Worry means we're trying to control situations. But that requires a lot of energy that has no positive outcome. Decide when you will worry: when you're sitting in a specific chair . . . in the shower . . . at a designated time, like between 6:00 and 6:15 each evening.

Focus on your surroundings and find the beauty there. Let the warmth of a fireplace, the beauty of a first snowfall, or the angelic face of an elderly person touch your heart.

Laugh. And then laugh some more. Then laugh again. Exercise your lungs, and bring the gift of life and humor to every waking moment of your life.

Choose to be a happy person. Find the positive in any situation.

Celebrate as often as you can. Birthdays, anniversaries, and other significant days that hold special meanings do not need to be celebrated only once a year. Find a reason to throw a party.

Anne Bryan Smollin, C.S.J.

is an international lecturer on wellness and spirituality. An educator and therapist, she holds a Ph.D. in Counseling from Walden University in Florida and is presently Executive Director of the Counseling for Laity center in Albany, New York. She is also the author of *Live, Laugh, and Be Blessed* (Sorin Books, 2006) and *God Knows You're Stressed* (Sorin Books, 2001).